Straight Ahead Jazz Fakebook

GERARD AND SARZIN
PUBLISHING CO.

Brooklyn, New York

Cover design by Ariev & Ariev
Front cover photo: © David Grogan
Back cover photo: © Cheung Ching Ming

Gerard & Sarzin Publishing Co.
146 Bergen Street
Brooklyn, N.Y. 11217

Printed on acid-free paper in the United States of America
ISBN 0-9628467-4-0 $25 softcover

Table of Contents

Introduction

Straight ahead is a term jazz musicians use in a variety of contexts. When jazz musicians describe a rhythm section as straight ahead, they are alluding to a drummer playing the typical *chang chang che chang* cymbal figure and a "walking" bassist supporting the groove with quarter notes and a few triplet figures thrown in for contrast. For at least half of an evening's performance, the rhythm section is in a swing mode. The drummer is playing the characteristic ride cymbal figure, the bassist is walking, and triplets are the dominant rhythm. Interspersed are a few pieces, or sections within pieces, based on Latin and funk rhythms.

Although musicians may not explicitly label it as such, it is easy to speak of straight ahead jazz instrumentation—acoustic bass, a drumset with a small bass drum and instruments suitable for bebop such as saxophone, trumpet and acoustic piano. Like other labels, straight ahead tells more about what it is not rather than what it is. Since the 1970s, the term has been used to distinguish contemporary jazz that is neither jazz-rock (fusion) nor avant-garde (free) jazz. For example, straight ahead jazz does not refer to the music of Spyro Gyra, David Sanborn, Ornette Coleman, the World Saxophone Quartet, or Cecil Taylor. With some minor quibbling, most jazz critics would agree that the composers represented in this collection write in a straight ahead style.

Straight ahead jazz has a few characteristic structural components. A straight ahead jazz melody is often modeled on the formats of American popular songs of the pre-rock era. The most typical is a 32-measure structure with an eight-measure theme (A) repeated, followed by a contrasting passage (B) called the bridge and a reprise of the A theme. The typical straight ahead jazz performance consists of a melody followed by improvisation on its chord changes. After the improvised solos, the melody is repeated. In several compositions, the melody is followed by a reprise of the introduction. Some of the compositions in this book go beyond these structural bounds. But one gets the sense that these are variations upon the form, rather than a distinct new approach.

Many of the compositions in this book were recorded on the Blue Note label in the 1950s and 1960s. During this period, the label became the most important source of hard bop jazz by promoting the music of Art Blakey, Horace Silver and the former sidemen of these two musicians. By concentrating on this pool of talented musicians and giving them artistic freedom the Blue Note sound developed—a tough sound with a hard, driving beat.

I have included works by Hal Galper, Tom Harrell and Mulgrew Miller—three outstanding composers active in jazz today.

Some Editorial Comments

In contrast to most jazz fakebooks in which only the melody line appears, this book provides musicians with essential subsidiary lines so they can make these pieces sound the way they were recorded. The compositions are in lead sheet style, with chord changes placed above the measure. These changes are used for improvising. Substitute changes appearing between double staves are to be played only with the written music. Tom Harrell, Mulgrew Miller and Hal Galper supplied me with lead sheets. The rest of the pieces were transcribed from recordings. Almost all the compositions receive their first printing here.

Evan Sarzin and I wish to give special thanks to Jamey Aebersold, John McNeil and Carl Johnson of Music Publishing Services (New York City) for their invaluable help.

Charley Gerard, Editor
March, 1999

Appointment in Ghana

Jackie McLean

Gmin9
Gmin9
1
Gmin9
Gmin9
Gmin$^6_9$
Gmin$^6_9$
Gsus4
2
Gmin9
Gmin9
B
Gmin9
E7(♯9)
Gmin$^6_9$
Gmin$^6_9$
B♭Maj7/F
E7(♯9)
Fine
D7(♯9)
G13
Gmin9
E7(♯9)
D7(♯9)
G13
B♭Maj7/F
E7(♯9)
D7(♯9)
G13
D7(♯9)
G13
Gsus4
D.S. al Fine
take 2nd ending

Backup

Larry Young

quiet blues

Blues changes in F on solos.

A Ballad For Doll

Jackie McLean

Beyond All Limits

Woody Shaw

A♭min
Bmin
Bmin
Gmin
9/8 Afro feel
Gmin
Asus4
F♯sus4
E♭sus4
Csus4
swing
A
Cmin7
E♭7(♭9 ♭5)
A♭Maj7
A♭Maj7
Amin9
F7(♭9 ♭5)
B♭Maj7
B♭Maj7
A♭7
AMaj
Fmin
Fmin or E♭7
Fmin
Fmin

Blue Lace

Lee Morgan

After solos, D.C. al Coda.

Repeat and fade.

Bop Stew

Hal Galper

Fmin7
Bb7
Ebmin7
Dmin7
3
GØ7/Db
C7(b9)
F7
3
Bb7
Eb7
Bbmin7
3
Eb7
AbMaj7
Ab7
Db7
EbMaj7
3
Gmin7
C7
Fmin7
3
Bb7
EbMaj7
EbMaj7

Calling Miss Khadija

Lee Morgan

fast, count in two

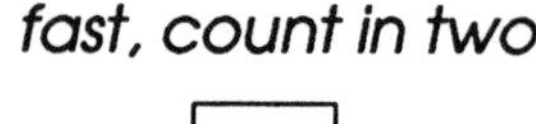

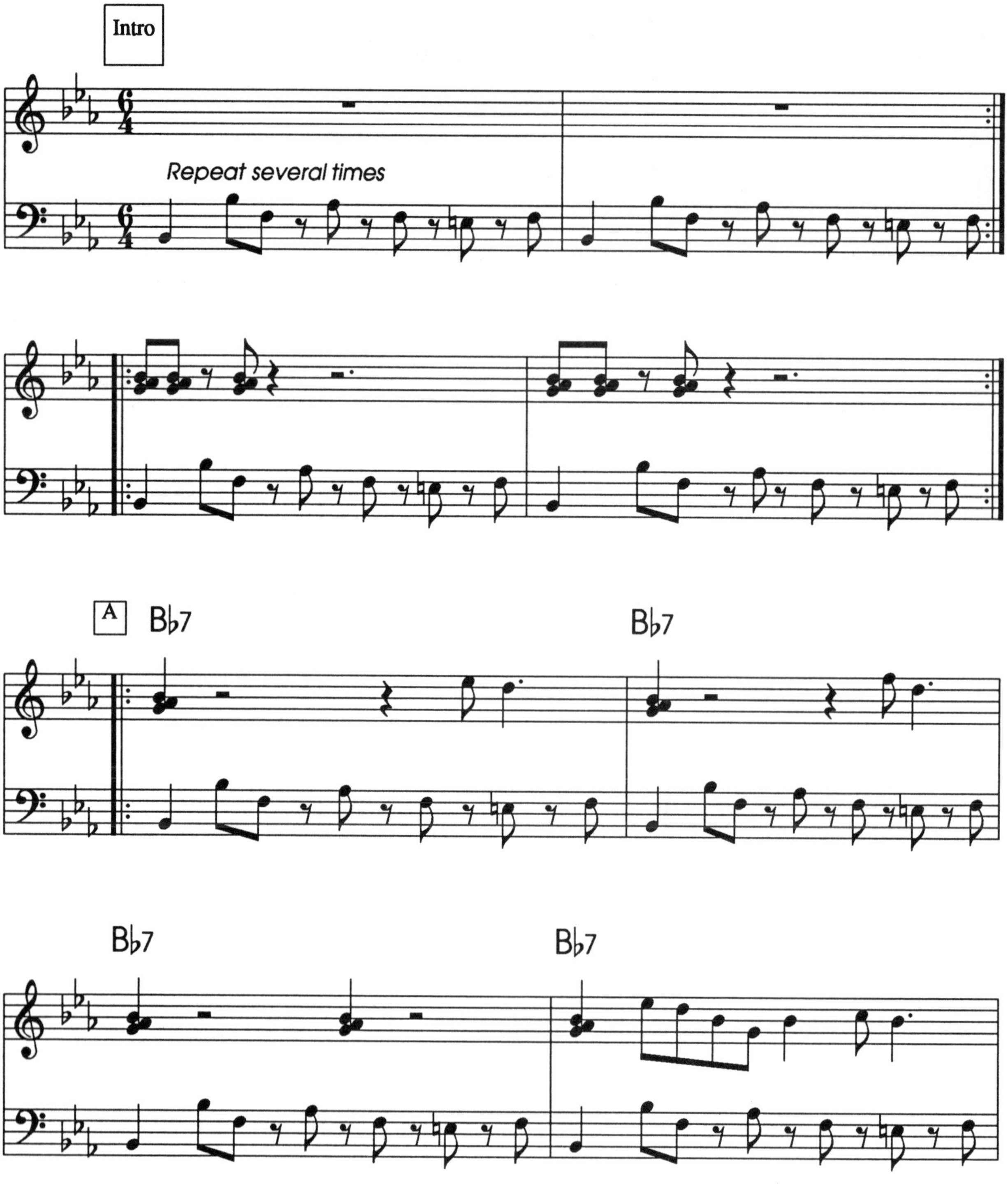
Intro
Repeat several times
A
B♭7
B♭7
B♭7
B♭7

E♭7
E♭7(♭5)
B♭7
B♭7
F7
E♭7
B♭7
B♭7

Caribbean Fire Dance

Joe Henderson

C♯7(♭9)
E♭Maj7
E7
A
A7(♯9)
E♭Maj7(♭5)
A7(♯9)
E♭Maj7(♭5)
A7(♯9)
E♭Maj7(♭5)
A7(♯9)
E♭Maj7(♭5)
A7(♯9)
E♭Maj7(♭5)
A7(♯9)
E♭Maj7(♭5)
A7(♯9)
E♭Maj7(♭5)
A7(♯9)
E♭Maj7(♭5)

Ceora

Lee Morgan

AbMaj7
Ebmin7 Ab7
DbMaj7
Dmin7 G7
Cmin7
F7(#9)
Bbmin7
Eb7
C∅7
F7
Bbmin7
Eb11
AbMaj7
Bbmin7
Eb7(b9)
After solos, D.C. al Coda.
Coda
Bbmin7
Eb7(b9)
AbMaj7
Bbmin7
Eb7(b9)
AbMaj7
Bbmin7
Eb7(b9)
AbMaj7

Cheesecake

Dexter Gordon

Cmin7
B
Gmin7
C7
Fmin7
B♭7
E♭min7
A♭7
Dmin
Dmin7
G7
3
A
Cmin
G7
Cmin
G7
Cmin
Cmin
3
Fmin
C7
Fmin
Fmin
Fmin
Dmin7
G7
Fmin7
B♭7
E♭min7
A♭7
Dmin7
G7
Cmin7
Cmin7

Cornbread

Lee Morgan

First solo is preceded by vamp. After solos, play tune and fade out on vamp.

Crisis

Freddie Hubbard

B7
B7
B♭7
B♭7
A7
F♯aug
Bmin7
F♯aug
Bmin7
1 Bmin7
2 Bmin7
B
G7
swing
C♯ø7
F♯aug
Bmin7
E7
Amin7
D7
A♭ø7
C♯7
F♯7
F♯7
D.S. al Coda
Coda
Bmin7

Do It Now

Brother Jack McDuff

jazz funk

Bass part is repeated without variation during solos. After tune is repeated, fade out on bass part.

The Egyptian

Curtis Fuller

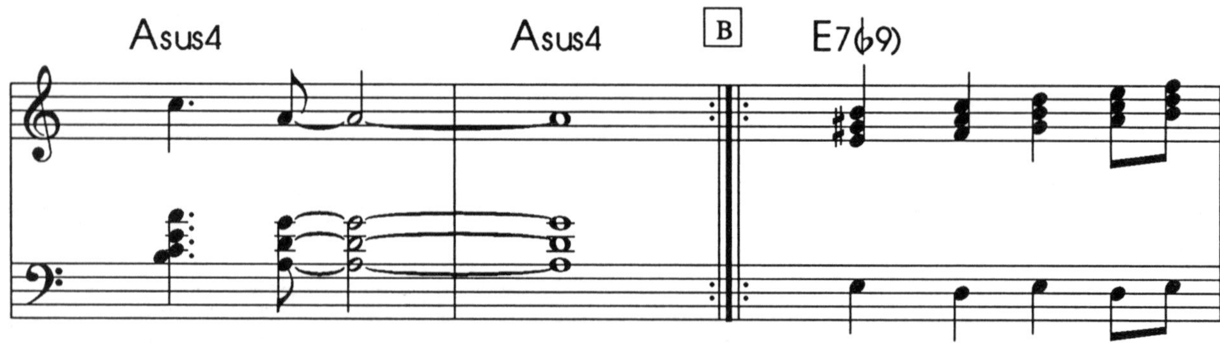

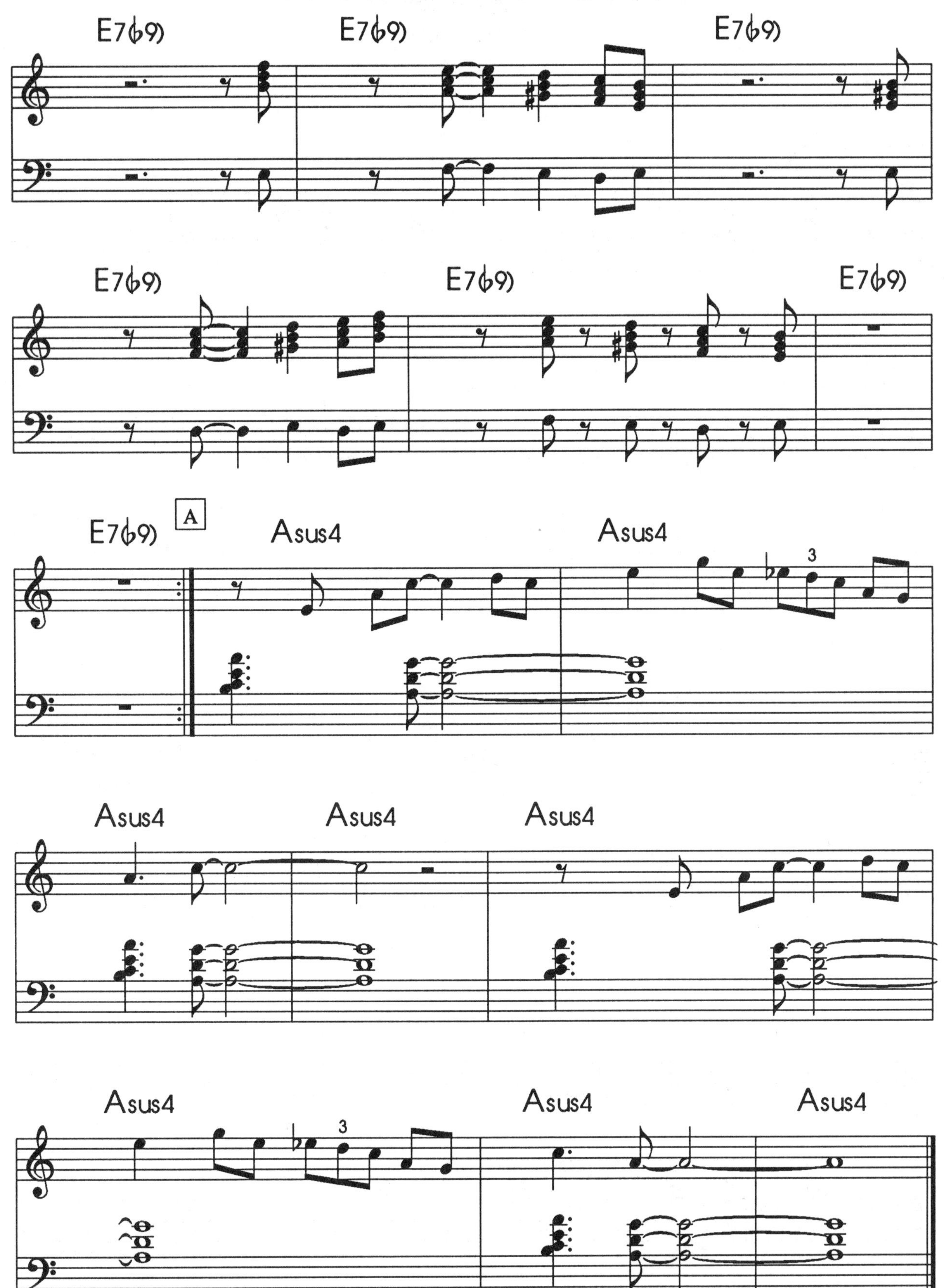
E7(♭9)
E7(♭9)
E7(♭9)
E7(♭9)
E7(♭9)
E7(♭9)
E7(♭9)
A
Asus4
Asus4
3
Asus4
Asus4
Asus4
Asus4
3
Asus4
Asus4

Expresso Bongo

Tom Harrell

Medium Fast Latin

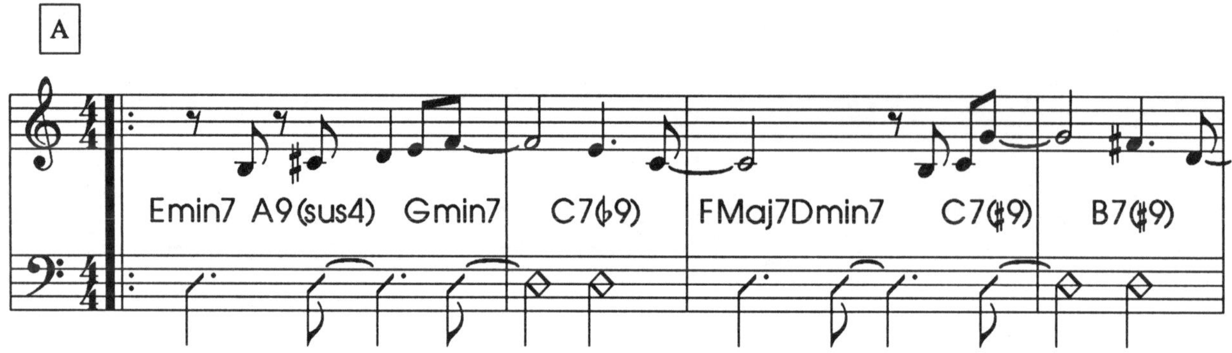

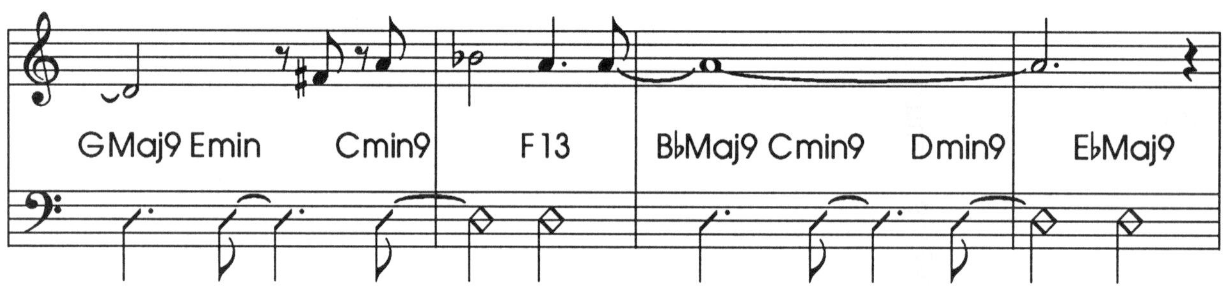

Bmin9 E9(sus4) A♭min9
D♭7(♭9)
G♭min9 C7(♭13 ♯9)
B7(♭13 ♯9)
C
Emin7 A9(sus4) Gmin9
C7(♭9)
FMaj9 Dmin9 C7(♯9)
B7(♯9)
GMaj9 Emin9 Cmin9
F13
G♭7(♭13 ♯9) C9(♯11) B7(♯9)
F13
D
Emin9 A9(sus4)
D♭ø7 G♭7(♯5)
Bmin9 Amin9 Gmin9
C9

After solos, D.C. al Coda.

Coda
Bmin9
Bmin6 B♭min9
Amin9
Amin6 Cmin9
Bmin9
Bmin6 B♭min9
Amin9
Amin6 Cmin9
Bmin9
Bmin6 B♭min9
Amin9
Amin6 Cmin9
Bmin9
Bmin6 B♭min9
Amin9
Amin6
DMaj/C
CMaj/B♭
BMaj/A

Figurine

Hal Galper

Most Like Lee

Lee Morgan

Five Will Get You Ten

Sonny Clark

E7(♯9 ♭5) F♯7(♯9 ♭5) E7(♯9 ♭5) D7(♯9 ♭5) Amin7 D7
A
Gmin7 Gmin7 A♭min7
C7 Gmin7 C7 Gmin7C7 D♭7
A♭min7 A♭min7 D♭7 Gmin7 C7
A♭min7 D♭7A♭min7D♭7 A♭min7D♭7 Gmin7 C7
FMaj7 FMaj7
Csus4 Csus4

For Those Who Do

Mulgrew Miller

Solos on B only. After solos, play entire tune. Then repeat B several times with piano solo and fade out on D11 chord.

Gotham Serenade

Hal Galper

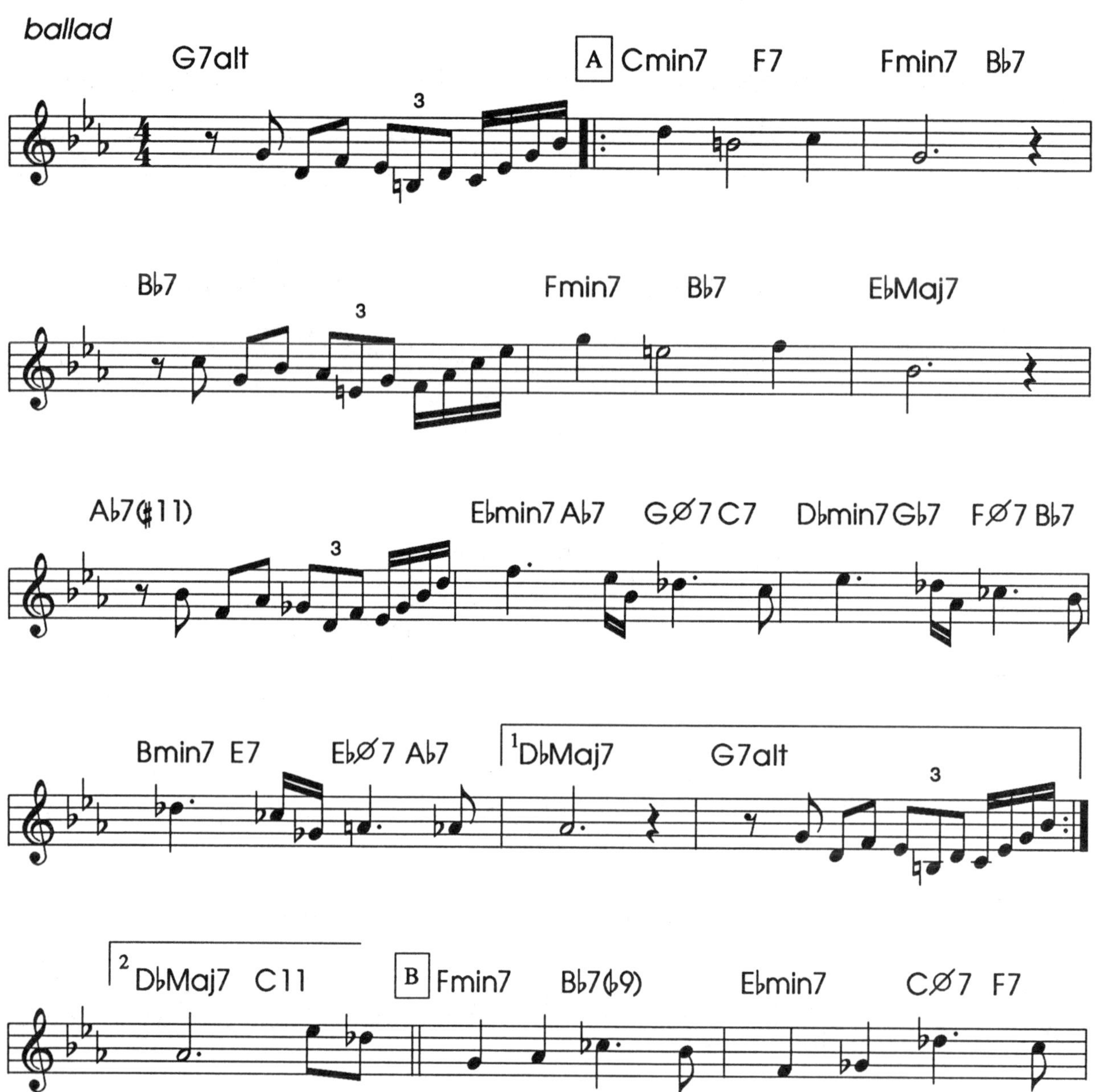

Bbmin7 Eb7
A7 Ebmin7/Ab Ab7
DbMaj7
Abmin7 Db7
G∅7
F#min(Maj7)
Fmin7
Bb7
A7(#11) Ab9
G7alt
G7alt
A
Cmin7
F7
Fmin7 Bb7
Bb7
Fmin7
Bb7
EbMaj7
Ab7(#11)
Ebmin7 Ab7
G∅7 C7
Dbmin7 Gb7
F∅7Bb7
Bmin7
E7
Eb∅7Ab7
Dbmin7
C7alt
Fine

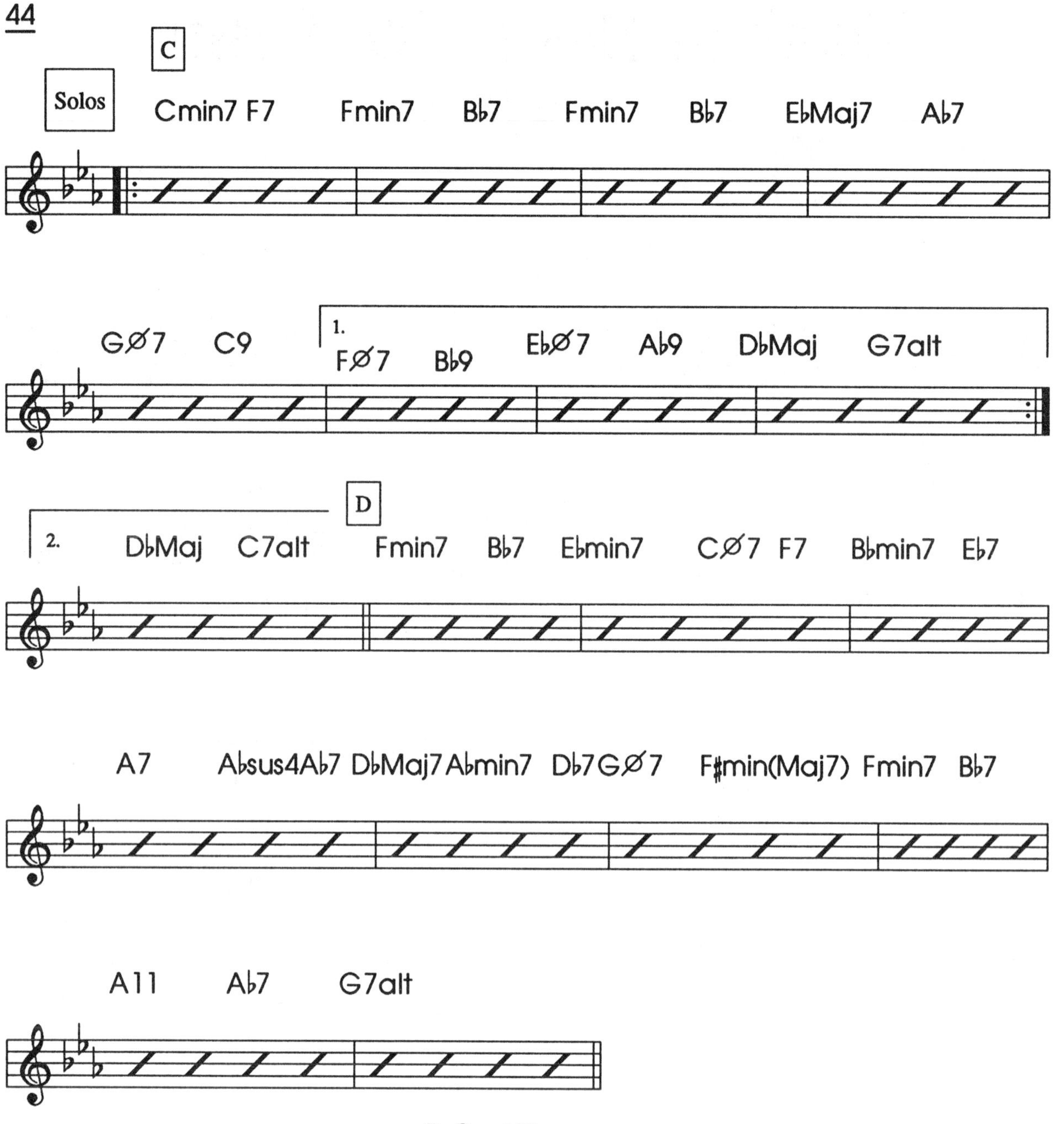
C
Solos
Cmin7 F7
Fmin7
Bb7
Fmin7
Bb7
EbMaj7
Ab7
GØ7
C9
1.
FØ7
Bb9
EbØ7
Ab9
DbMaj
G7alt
2.
DbMaj
C7alt
D
Fmin7
Bb7
Ebmin7
CØ7
F7
Bbmin7
Eb7
A7
Absus4Ab7
DbMaj7Abmin7
Db7GØ7
F#min(Maj7)
Fmin7
Bb7
A11
Ab7
G7alt

D.C. al Fine

Neither Here Nor There

Mulgrew Miller

Grew's Tune

Mulgrew Miller

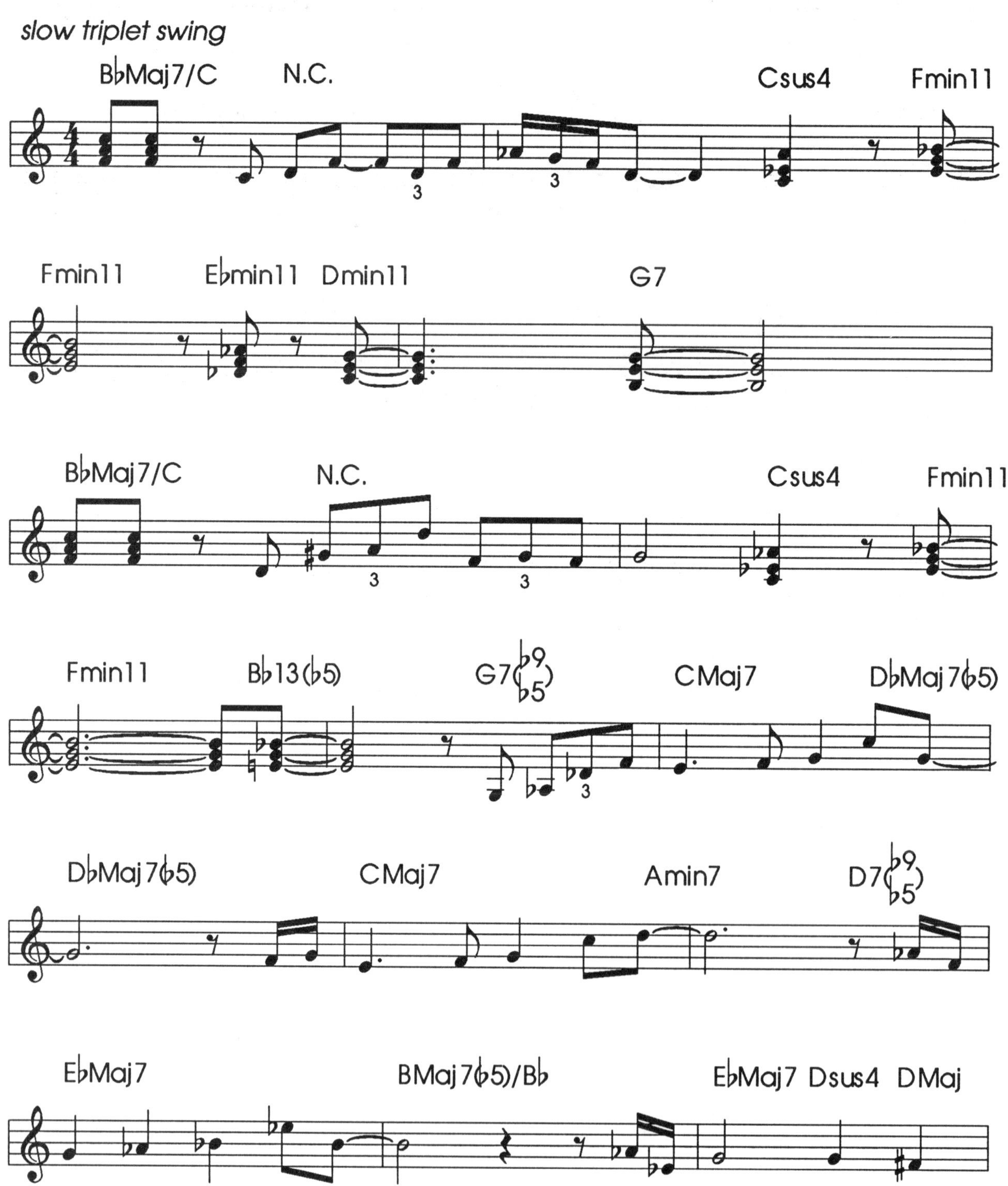

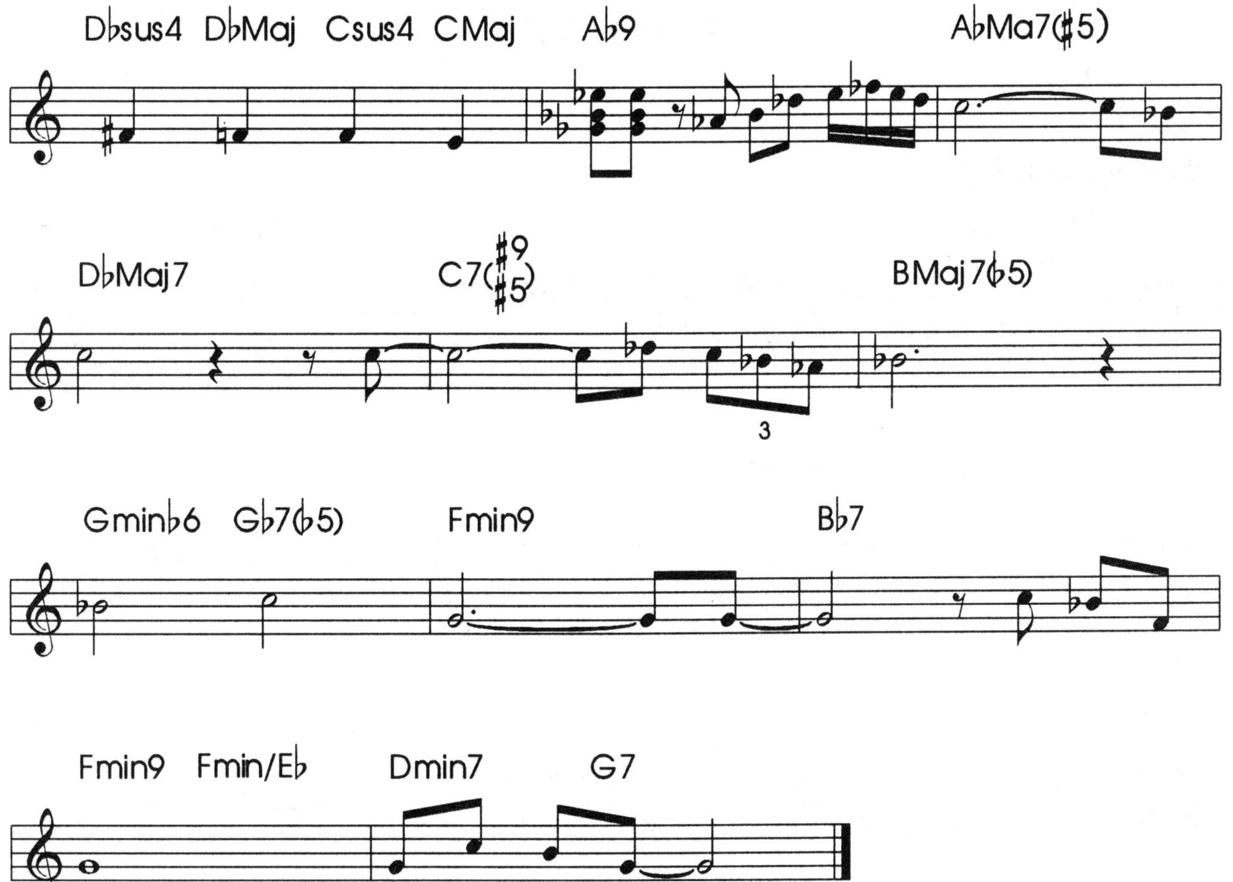
D♭sus4 D♭Maj Csus4 CMaj
A♭9
A♭Ma7(♯5)
D♭Maj7
C7(♯9 ♯5)
3
BMaj7(♭5)
Gmin♭6 G♭7(♭5)
Fmin9
B♭7
Fmin9 Fmin/E♭
Dmin7
G7

Hand In Hand

Mulgrew Miller

1

AbMaj/Bb AbMaj/Bb EbMaj/F

EbMaj/F

2

EbMaj/F D11

D11 Gmin7 Amin7 BbMaj7 Csus4 DbMa9

DbMa9 DbMa9

Hello Bright Sunflower

Duke Pearson

easy swing

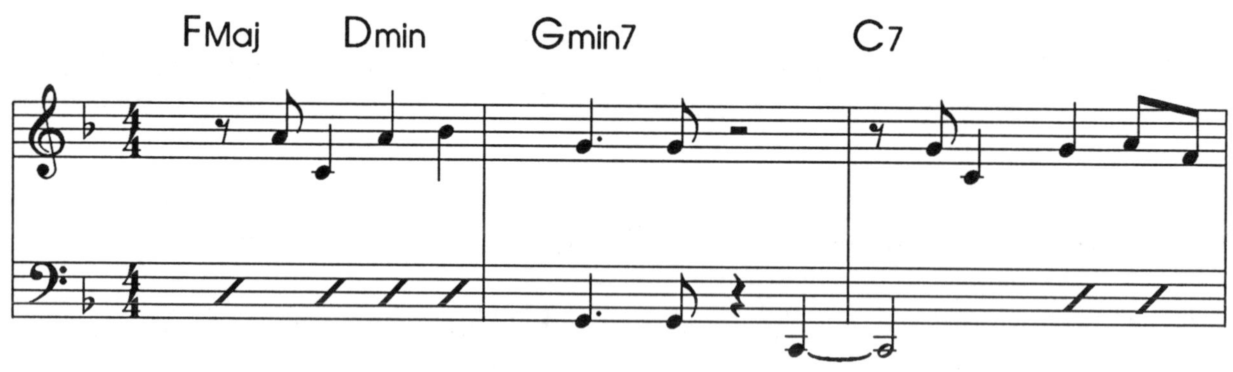

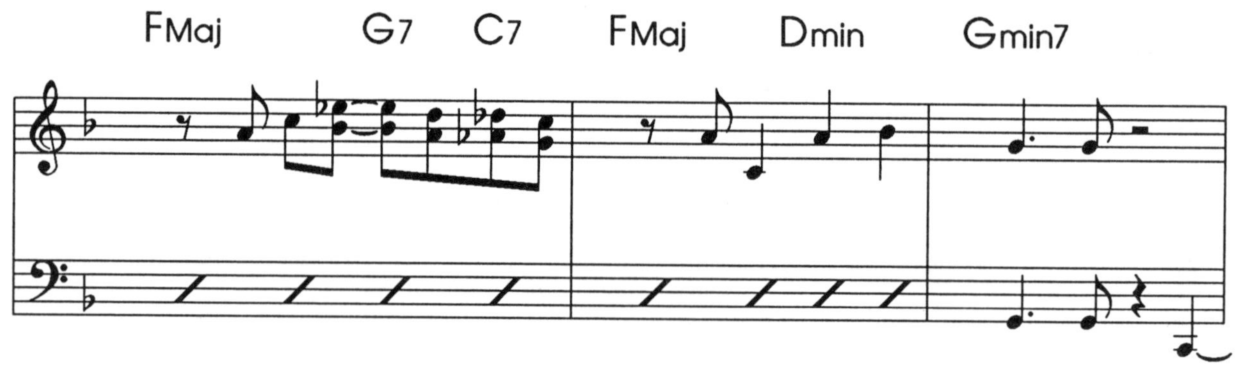

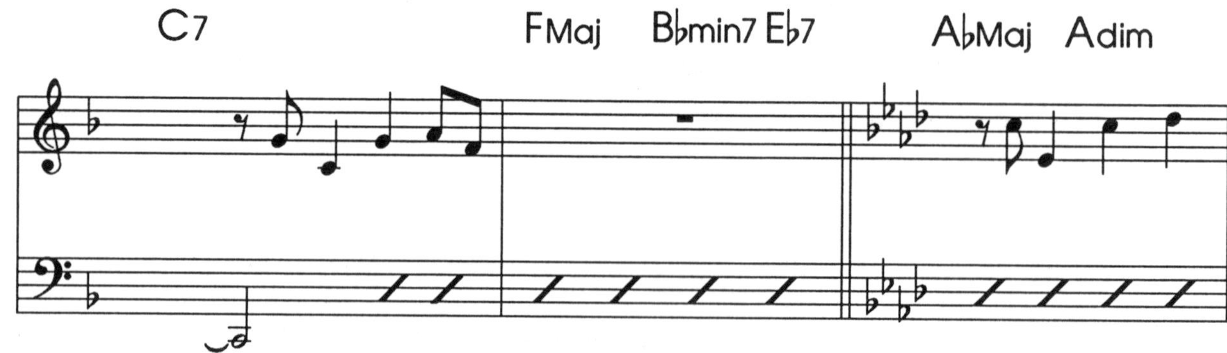

After solos, repeat tune, solo on the chord changes one more time and then fade out.

Hip Strut

Jackie McLean

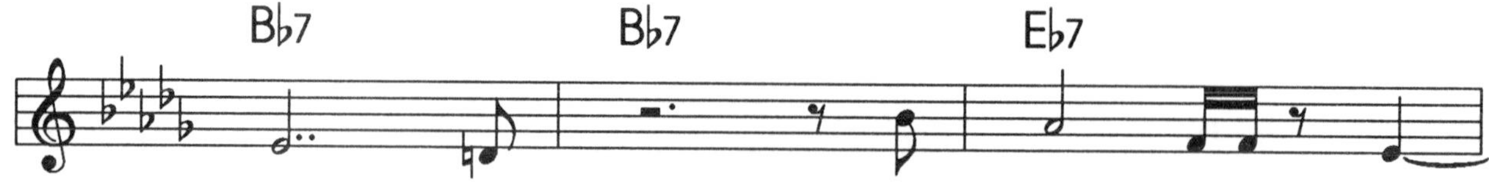

Solos: One chorus on blues changes (A) followed by one chorus on vamp (B).

Hub Cap

Freddie Hubbard

Gmin7
C7
FMaj7
Dbmin7
Gb7
BMaj7
Emin7
BMaj7
Cmin7
F7(b9)
A
Bbmin6
Cdim
F7(b9)
Bbmin6
CØ7
F7
Bbmin6
EbØ7
Ab7
C7(b9)F7
Bbmin6
DbMaj
C7(b9)
F7
Bbmin6
Bbmin6
Ebmin
Bbmin
Fine

Kozo's Waltz

Lee Morgan

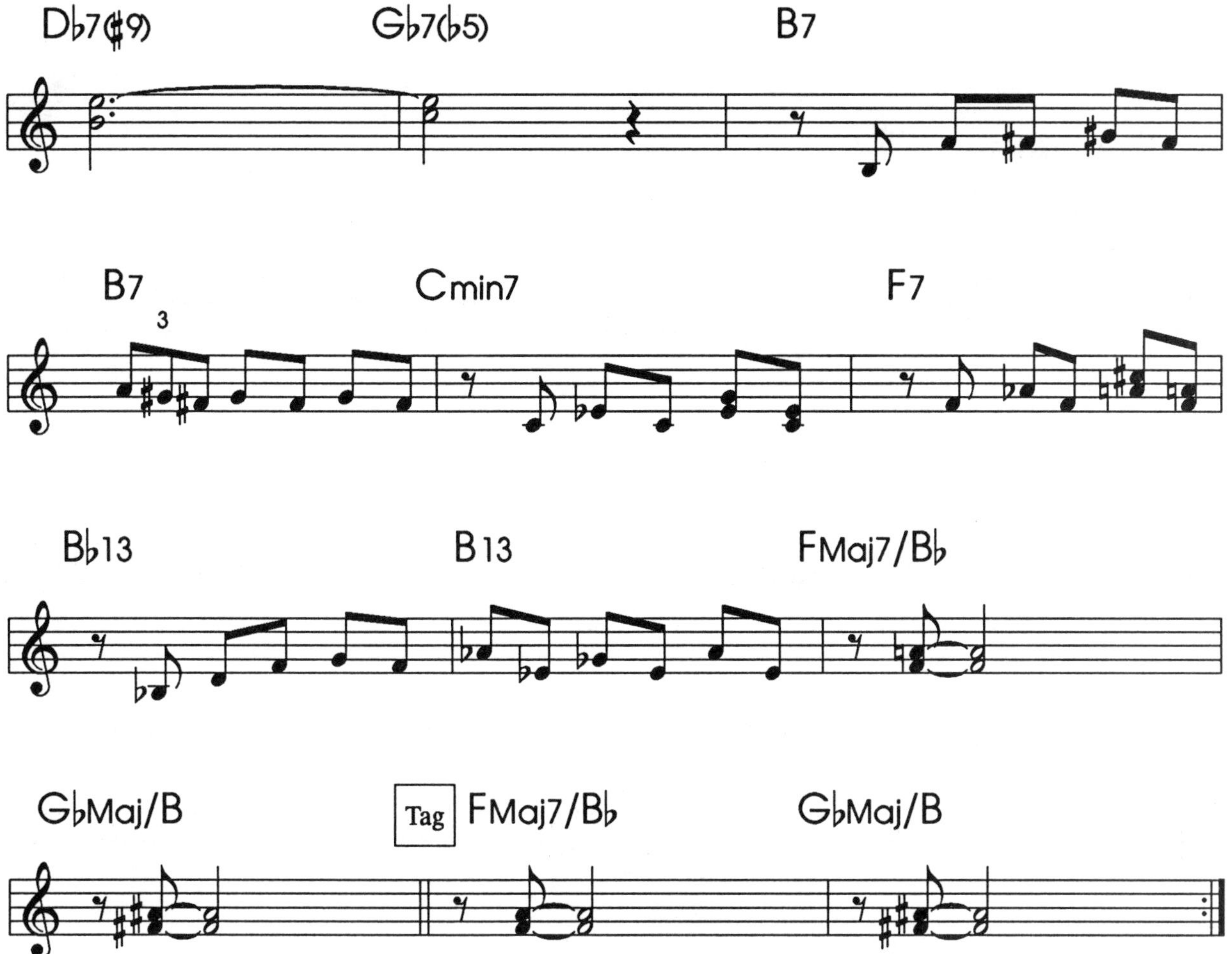

Solos on A chord changes.

Leilani's Leap

Mulgrew Miller

D♭7
C7(♯9)
F7
A1
Amin7
FMaj7
Amin7
FMaj7
E♭Maj
FMaj
GMaj
GMaj

Let's

Thad Jones

2
F7(♭5)
F7(♭5)
Drum Solo
Fine
Go to Solos

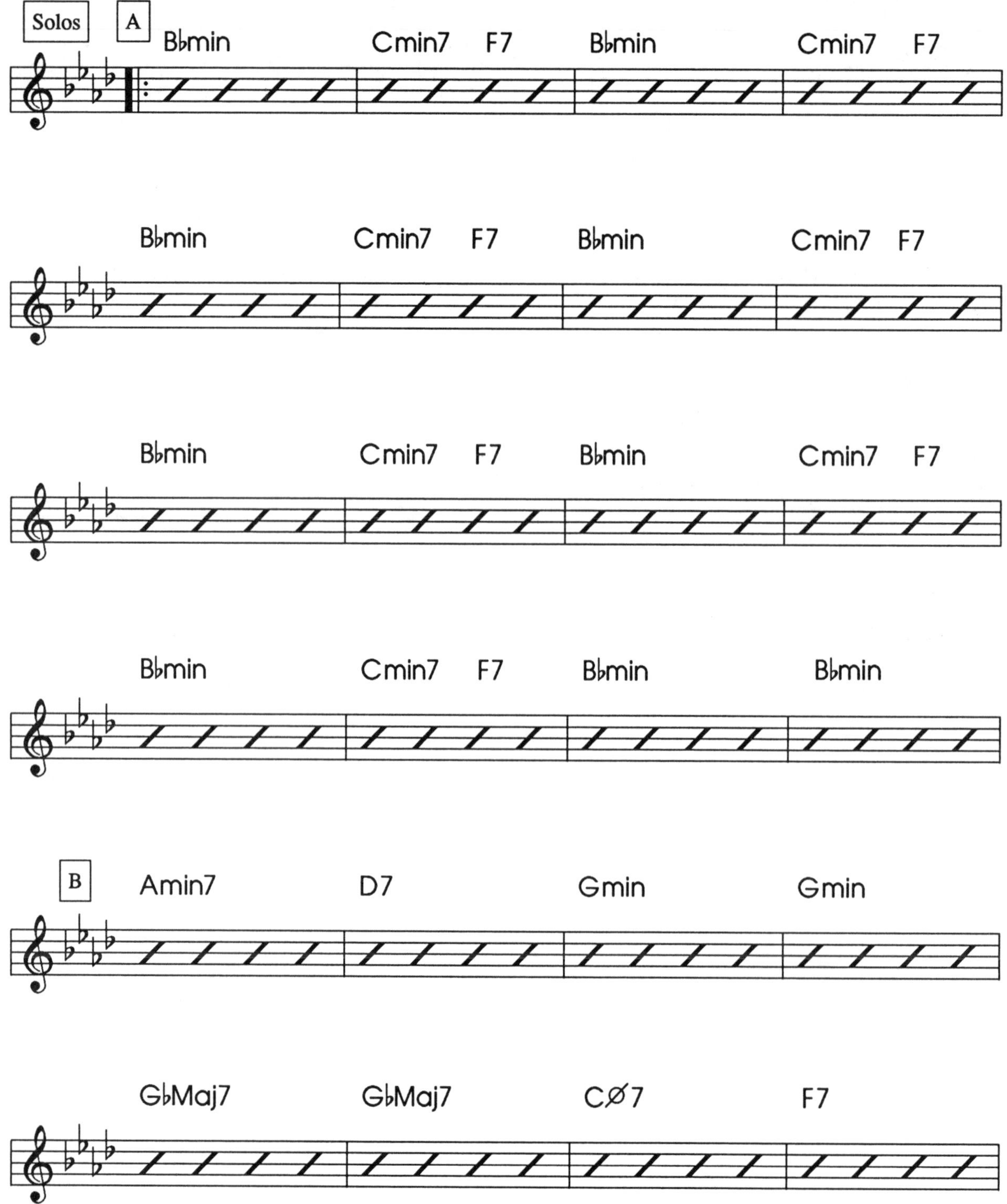
Solos
A
B♭min
Cmin7 F7
B♭min
Cmin7 F7
B♭min
Cmin7 F7
B♭min
Cmin7 F7
B♭min
Cmin7 F7
B♭min
Cmin7 F7
B♭min
Cmin7 F7
B♭min
B♭min
B
Amin7
D7
Gmin
Gmin
G♭Maj7
G♭Maj7
CØ7
F7

A
B♭min
Cmin7 F7
B♭min
Cmin7 F7

B♭min
Cmin7 F7
B♭min
1
Cmin7 F7

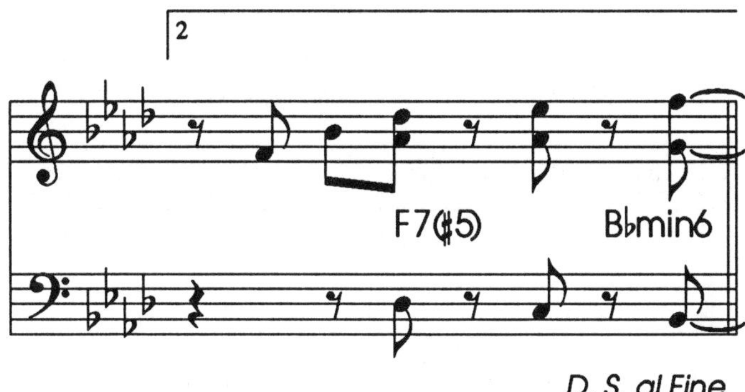
2
F7(♯5)
B♭min6
D. S. al Fine

Little B's Poem

Bobby Hutcherson

relaxed jazz waltz

Loose Change

Hal Galper

Luny Tune

Larry Young

Solos on "I Got Rhythm" chord changes in B♭.

Marie Antoinette

Wayne Shorter

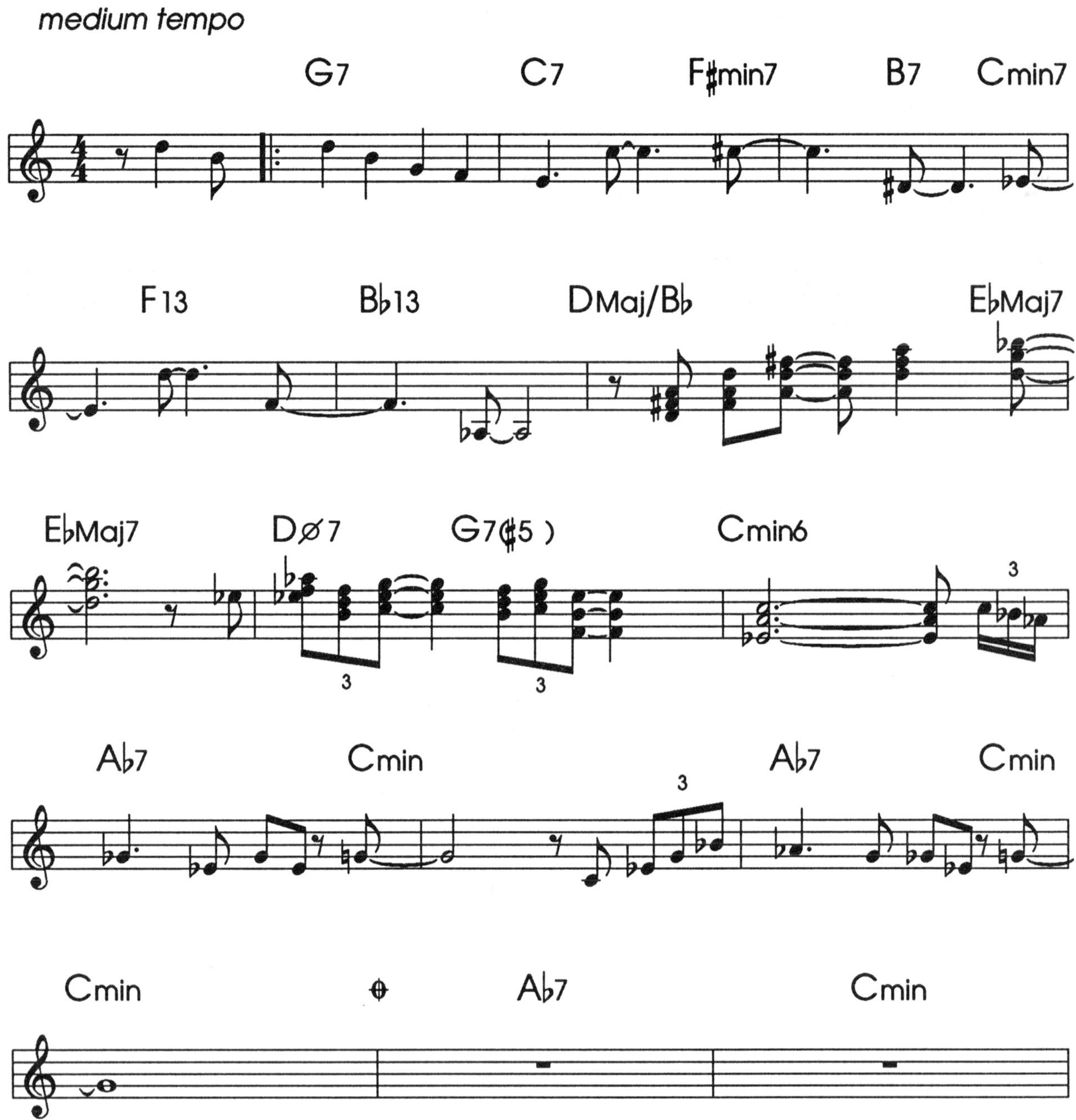

Piano solos during whole note rests.

After solos, D.C. al Coda.

Piano solos during Coda. Fade out.

Melody For Melonae

Jackie McLean

Between solos, play B. After solos, repeat B then repeat A al Fine.

Minor Apprehension

Jackie McLean

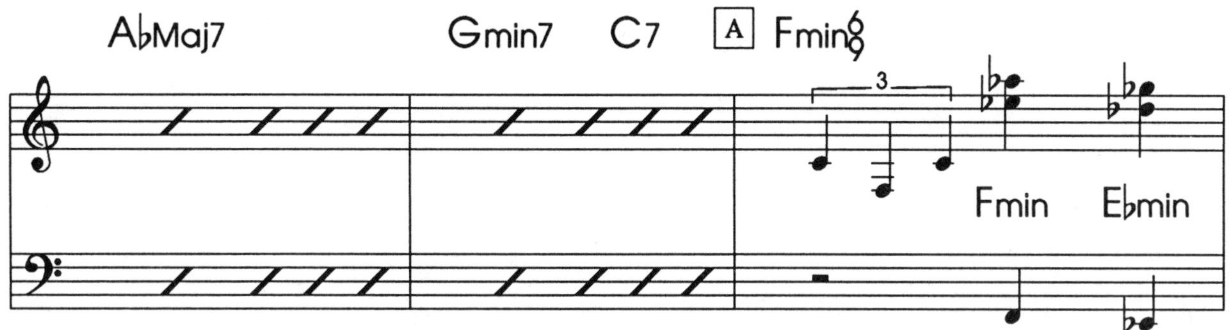
A♭Maj7
Gmin7
C7
A
Fmin6/9
3
Fmin
E♭min

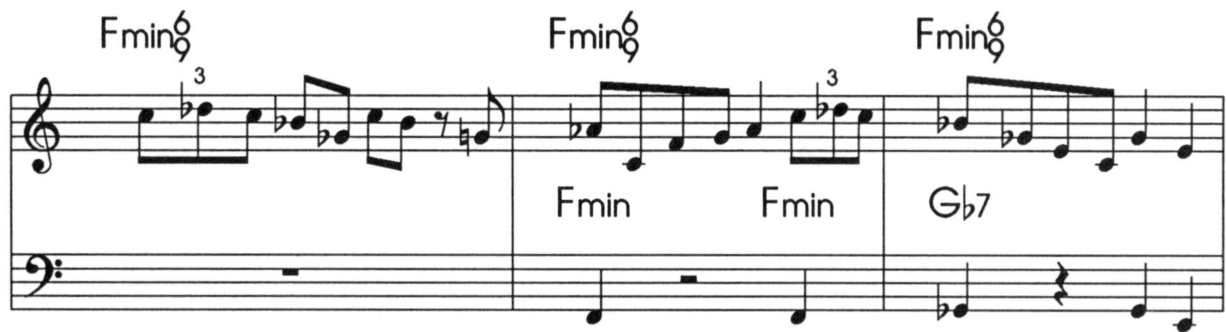
Fmin6/9
3
Fmin6/9
3
Fmin6/9
Fmin
Fmin
G♭7

Fmin6/9
Fmin6/9
3
Fmin6/9
Fmin6/9
Fmin

Moontrane

Woody Shaw

2
Fmin
B♭7
B
E♭Maj7
Fmin7
B♭7
E♭Maj7
E♭Maj7
Amin7
D7
Gmin
Fmin
B♭min
A♭min
C♯min
Bmin
Bmin
A
B♭Maj7(♭5)
B♭Maj7(♭5)
3
Amin7
3
Amin7
Cmin6/9
3
Fsus4
B♭6/9
E♭Maj7(♭5)
DMaj7
DMaj7

Mutt & Jeff

Brother Jack McDuff

Cmin6
N.C.
Ab7
Ab7
Ab7
Ab7
D7(#9)
G7(b5)
Cmin6
Cmin6
N.C.
A
G in bass throughout A

Solos

C A♭Maj7(♯5)/G | A♭Maj7(♯5)/G | E♭Maj7(♯5)/G | E♭Maj7(♯5)/G

A♭Maj7(♯5)/G | F♯Maj7(♯5)/G EMaj7(♯5)/G | E♭Maj7(♯5)/G | E♭Maj7(♯5)/G

D♭Maj7/G | D♭Maj7/G | D♭Maj7/G | D♭Maj7/G

CMaj7/G | CMaj7/G D♭Maj7/G | CMaj7/G | CMaj7/G

D Fmin7 | B♭7 | E♭Maj7 | A♭7

Dmin7 | G7 | Cmin6 | 1 C7

2 Cmin6 | C A♭Maj7(♯5)/G | A♭Maj7(♯5)/G | E♭Maj7(♯5)/G

EbMaj7(#5)/G
AbMaj7(#5)/G
F#Maj7(#5)/G
EMaj7(#5)/G
EbMaj7(#5)/G
EbMaj7(#5)/G
DbMaj7/G
DbMaj7/G
DbMaj7/G
DbMaj7/G
CMaj7/G
CMaj7/G
DbMaj7/G
CMaj7/G
CMaj7/G
D.S. al Coda
Coda
Ab7
Ab7
Ab7
Ab7
D7(#9)
G7(b5)
N.C.
3
3
Cmin6
sustain chord

New Monastery

Andrew Hill

slow triplet feel

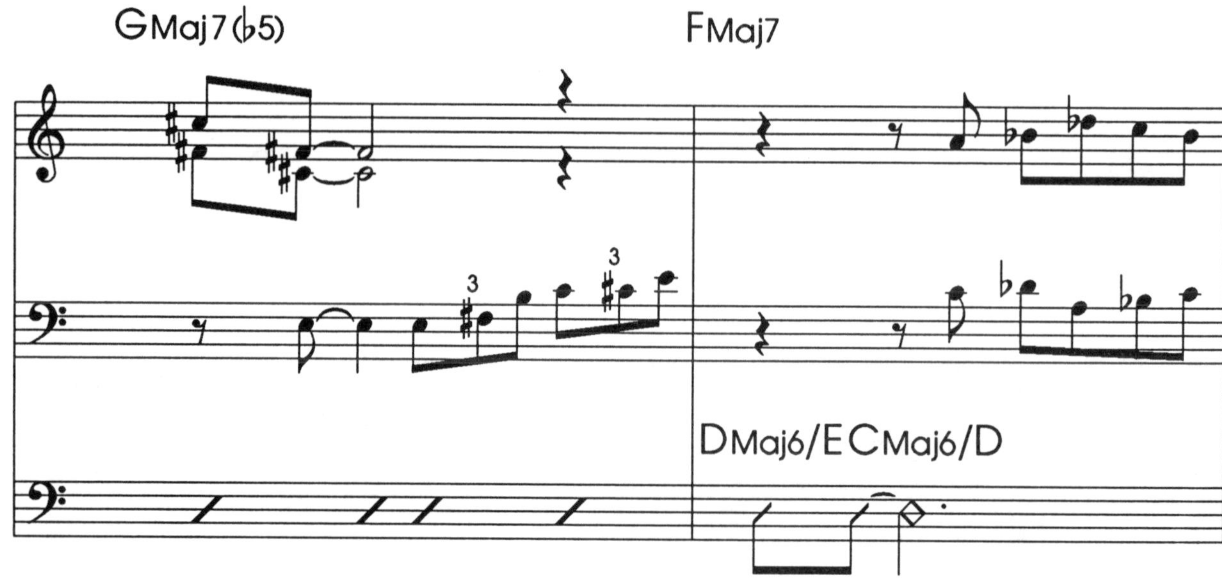

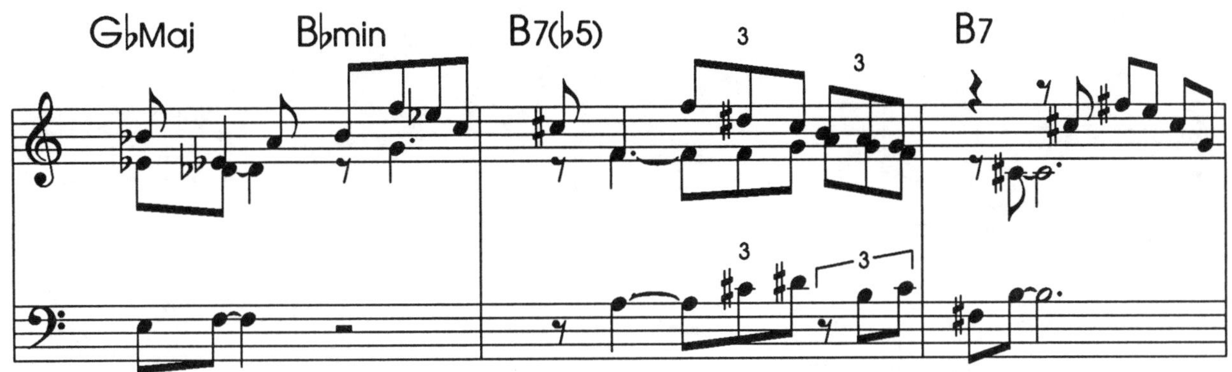
G♭Maj
B♭min
B7(♭5)
B7
3
3
3
3

B7
CMaj7(♭5)
A♭min6
3
3
3
3

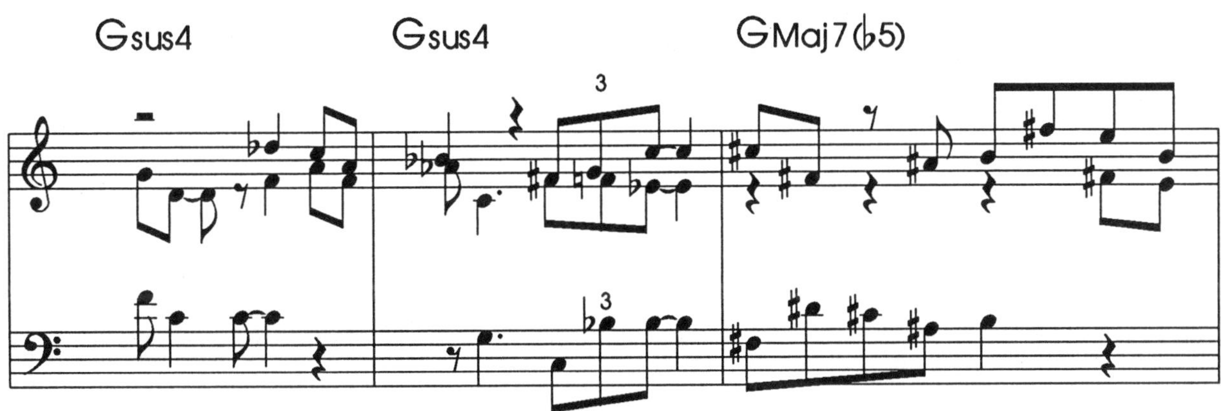
Gsus4
Gsus4
GMaj7(♭5)
3
3

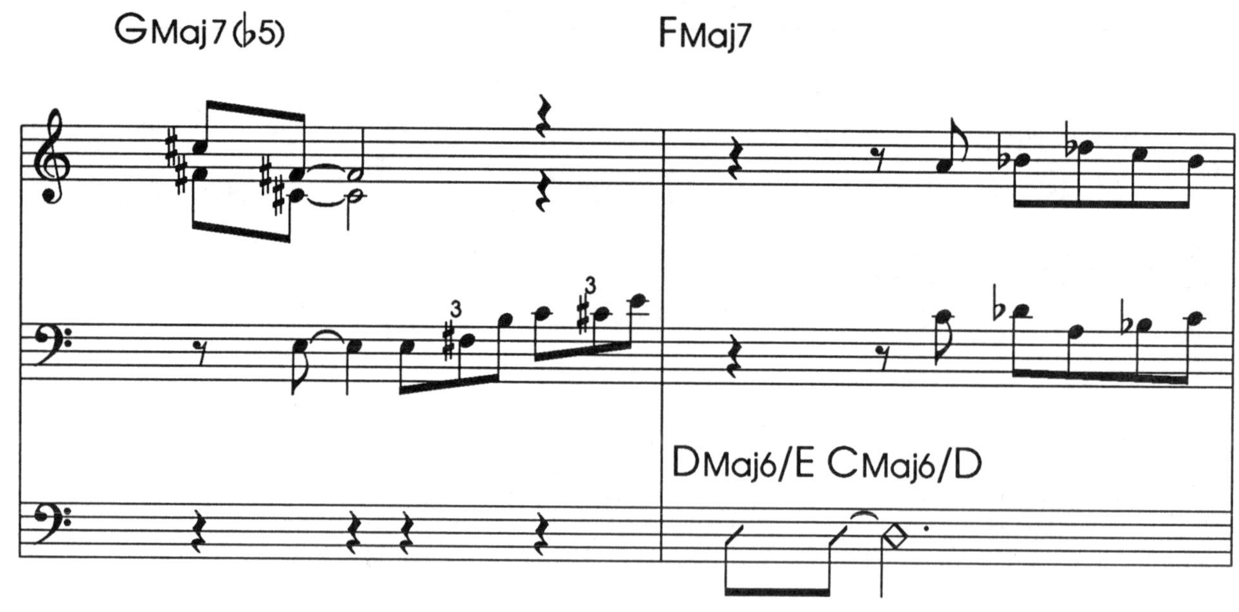
GMaj7(♭5)
FMaj7
3
3
DMaj6/E CMaj6/D

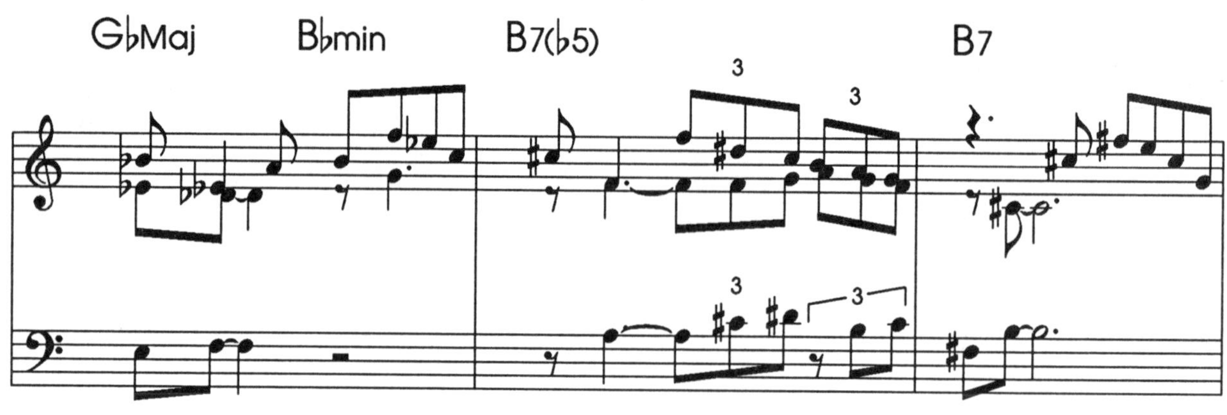
G♭Maj
B♭min
B7(♭5)
B7
3
3
3
3

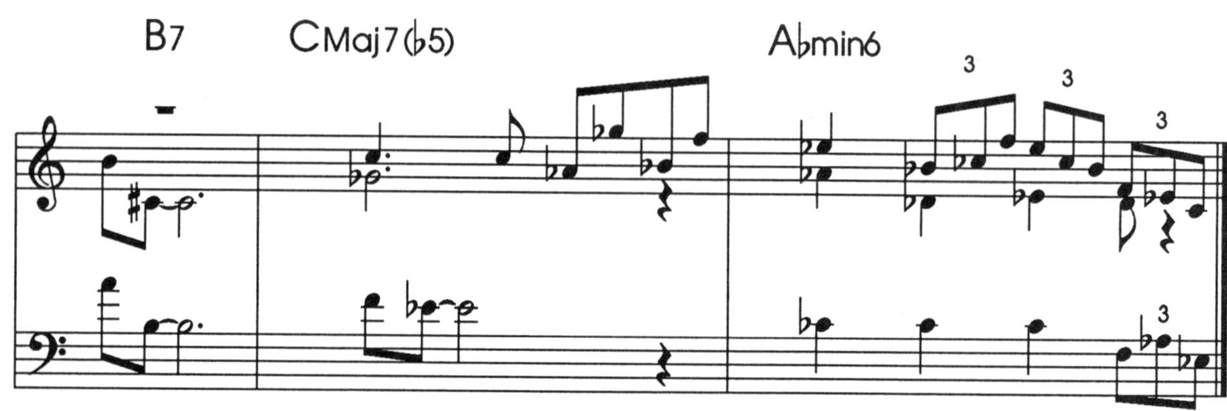
B7
CMaj7(♭5)
A♭min6
3
3
3
3

Return Trip

Mulgrew Miller

Our Thing

Joe Henderson

B♭Maj7
E♭min7
A♭7
D♭min
3
3

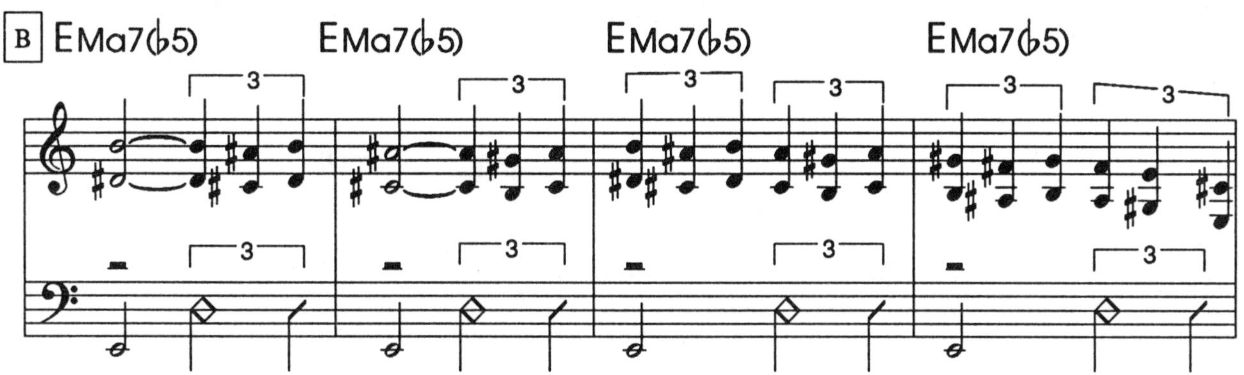

B
EMa7(♭5)
EMa7(♭5)
EMa7(♭5)
EMa7(♭5)
3

E♭m9
E♭m9
E♭m9
E♭m9
2nd voice continues
on lower stave

EMa7(♭5)
EMa7(♭5)
EMa7(♭5)
Piano follows rhythmic pattern
for E7(♭5) as above.
3

EMa7(♭5)
F9
F9
Piano continues 6/8 rhythmic feel until B♭mi7 chord.
F9
F9
A2
B♭Maj7
A♭min7
D♭7
G♭Maj7
F7
B♭min7
A♭min7
G♭Maj7
F7
B♭Maj7
G♭Maj7
F7
B♭min

The average man doesn't want to use his brain when he listens to music. Music should wash away the dust of his everyday life. He doesn't want to figure out what the musicians are doing. He's been figuring things out all day. He wants to get away from that and be taken out of this world. Music is entertainment.

• Art Blakey

Notes and Tones by Arthur Taylor. (Perigee Books, N.Y., 1982)

Paris Eyes

Larry Young

F6/9
E♭6/9
E7
E♭7
F6/9
F6/9
E♭6/9
E♭6/9
E7
A♭Maj7
Gmin7
C7
A
FMaj7
Gmin7/F
FMaj7
FMaj7
E♭Maj7
DMaj7
CMaj7
D♭Maj7
C7
FMaj7

Portrait of a Mountain

Mulgrew Miller

D♭Maj7
D♭Maj7
EMaj7
EMaj7
D♭Maj7
FMaj7
E♭Maj7
DMaj/G
FMaj7
A♭Maj7
GMaj7
D13(♯11)
A
B Locrian
B Locrian
FMaj/F♯
FMaj/F♯
FMaj7
FMaj7
AMaj/B♭
AMaj/B♭
CMaj7/D
D7(♭13 ♯9)
A♭Maj7
CMaj/A♭
B♭Maj/G♭
CMaj/A♭
AMaj7
D♭Maj7
E♭Maj7
E♭Maj7
BMaj7
BMaj7
A6/9
A♭6/9
A♭6/9

Promethean

Mulgrew Miller

Solos are based on the A section of the pop standard, "Days of Wine and Roses" in F.

Refuge

Andrew Hill

D7(♭5)
D7(♭5)
C7(♭5)
C7(♭5)
G♭7(♭5)
G♭7(♭5)
8va
E♭sus4
E♭sus4
D♭Ma7(♭5)
D♭Ma7(♭5)
E7
E7
Esus4 E7 Esus4 E7
Esus4 E7 Esus4 E7

Right Now

Charles Tolliver

1 E♭7(♭5)
2 E♭7(♭5) E7(♯5)
B
FMaj7
F7 E7
E♭7
Bmin7 E7 AMaj7 A∅7 D7(♯9) G7
G7 F7 G7
A
E♭7(♭5) E♭7(♭5)
F7 E7
E♭7
F7 E7
E♭7(♭5) E♭7(♭5) E♭7(♭5)
E♭7
F7 E7
E♭7
E♭7(♭5) E♭7(♭5) E♭7(♭5)
F7 E7
E♭7
F7 E7

Ritha

Larry Young

Ab7 D7 GMaj7
Ab7
GMaj7
A
A13
Ab13
DbMaj7
G7
Cmin
A∅7
D7
GMaj7
Bb7
EbMaj7
A13
F#13
B13
EMaj7
G13
CMaj7
CMaj7

Sail Away

Tom Harrell

EMaj7(♯5)
AMaj7
E♭min7
A♭9(sus4)
B9(sus4)
3
E
B♭min7
3
E♭7(♭9 ♯9)
E13(sus4)
E13(♭9)
AMaj7
3
F♯min11
D13(sus4)
C13(sus4)
B♭13(sus4)
G7(♯5 ♯9)
F
Emin7
A7(♯5 ♯9)
Dmin7
G7(♭9 sus4)
CMaj7
Amin9
CMaj7/G
F♯min7
B7(♯5 ♯9)
G
B♭Maj7(6 9)
A7(♯5 ♯9)
Dmin7
G13(sus4)
G7(♯11 ♭9)
last time
Emin7/G
G13(sus4)
Emin7/G
G13(sus4)

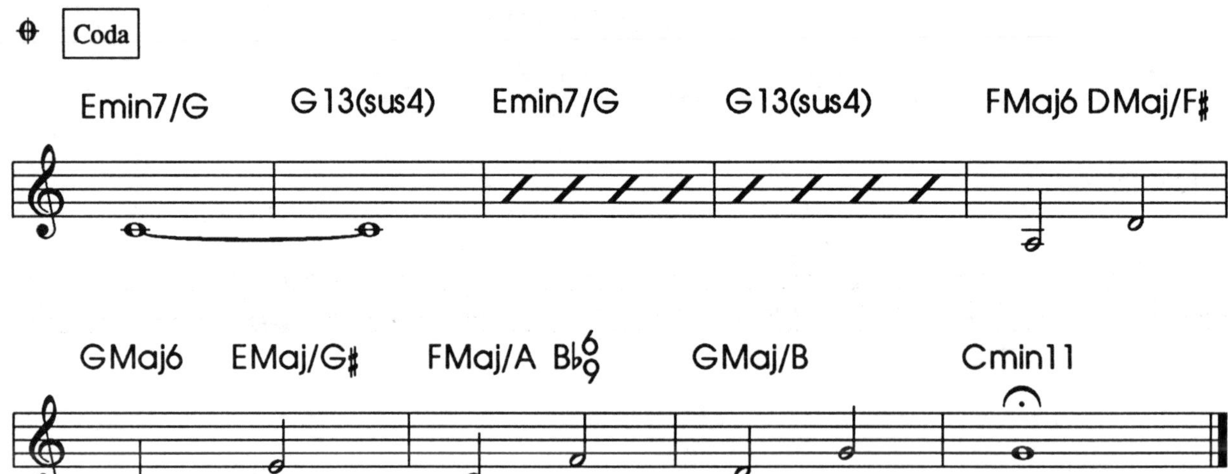
Coda
Emin7/G
G13(sus4)
Emin7/G
G13(sus4)
FMaj6 DMaj/F♯
GMaj6
EMaj/G♯
FMaj/A
B♭6/9
GMaj/B
Cmin11

Teeter Totter

Joe Henderson

Sakeena's Vision

Wayne Shorter

medium tempo

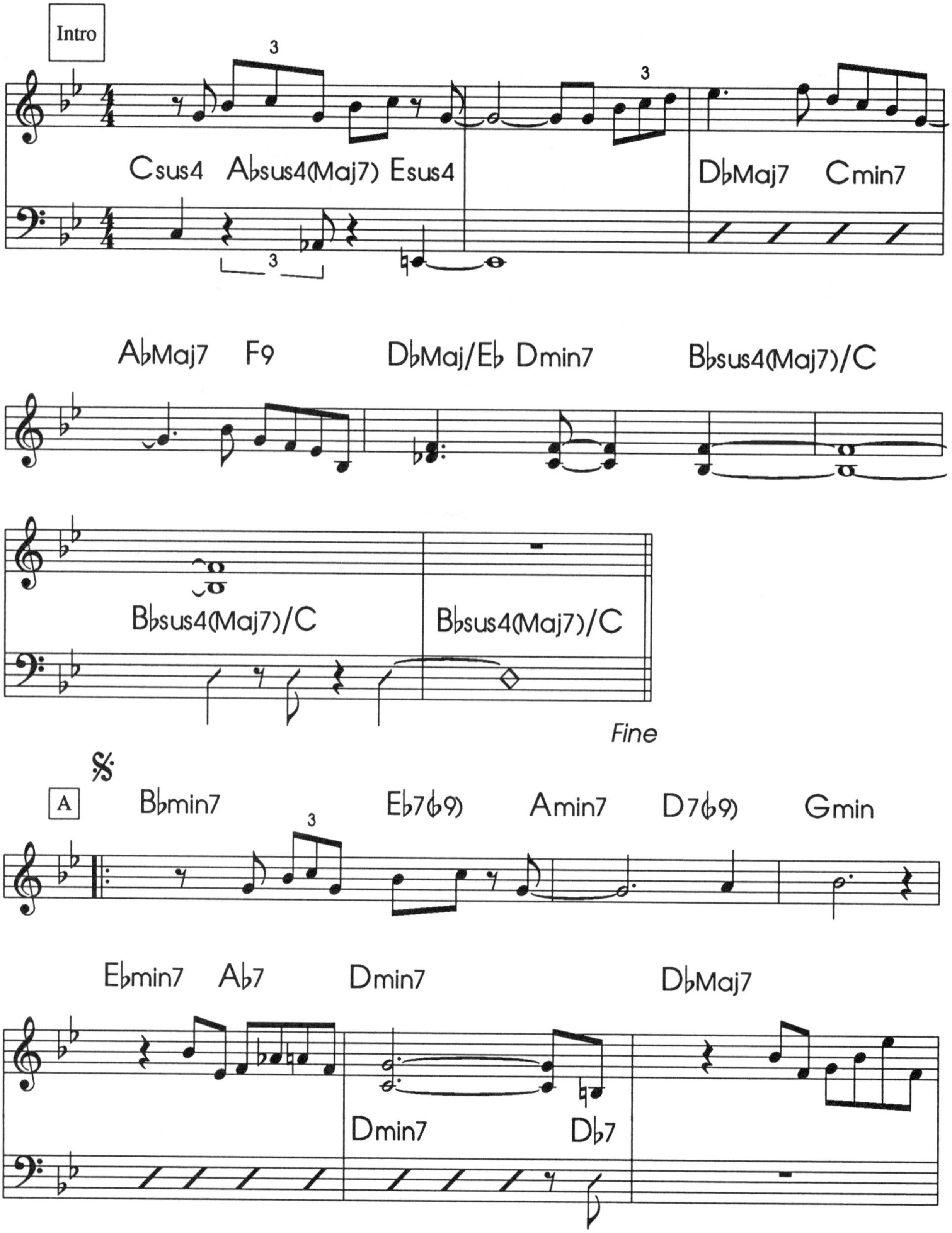

Intro

Csus4 A♭sus4(Maj7) Esus4

D♭Maj7 Cmin7

A♭Maj7 F9 D♭Maj/E♭ Dmin7 B♭sus4(Maj7)/C

B♭sus4(Maj7)/C

B♭sus4(Maj7)/C

Fine

A

B♭min7 E♭7(♭9) Amin7 D7(♭9) Gmin

E♭min7 A♭7 Dmin7 D♭Maj7

Dmin7 D♭7

Solo on AABA chord changes. After solos, repeat tune, then D.C. al Fine.

Scene

Tom Harrell

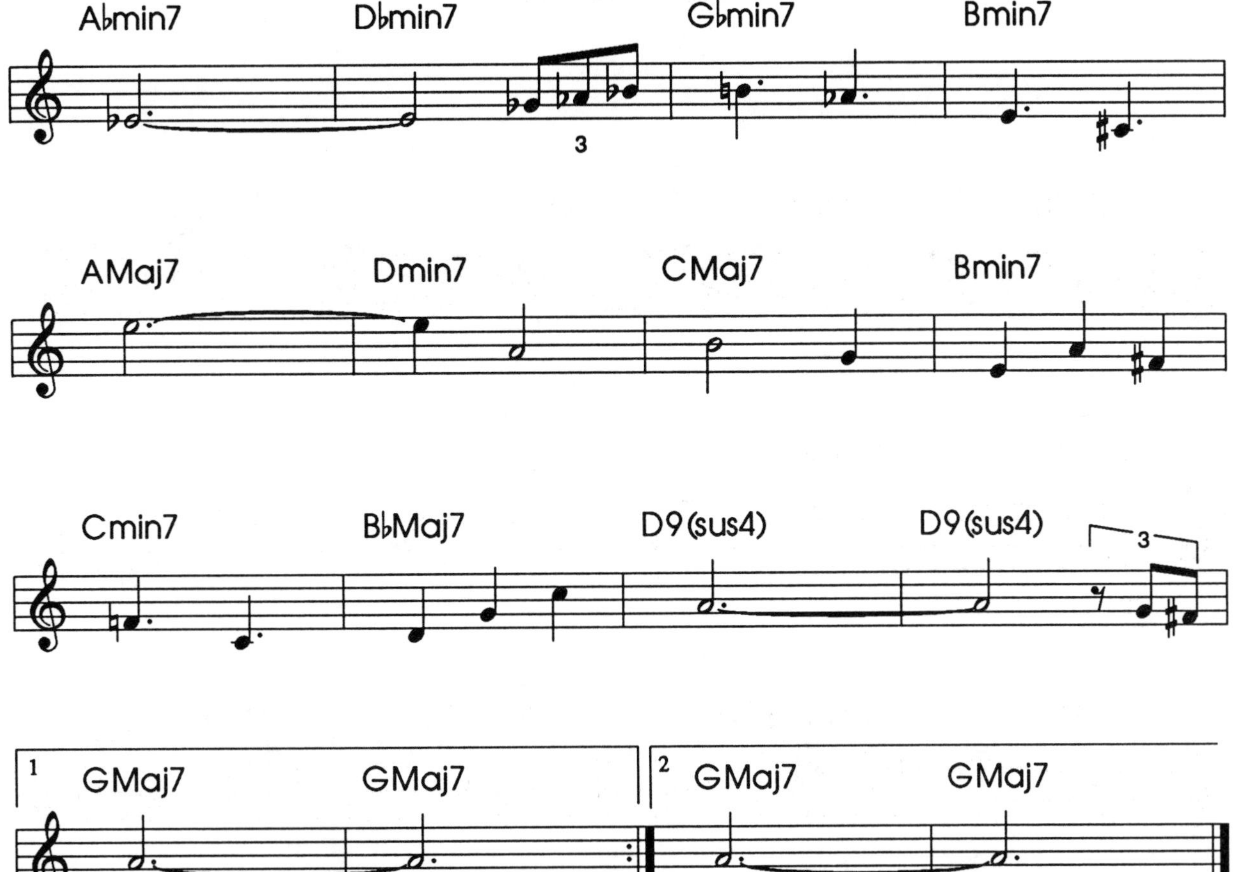

A♭min7
D♭min7
G♭min7
Bmin7
3
AMaj7
Dmin7
CMaj7
Bmin7
Cmin7
B♭Maj7
D9(sus4)
D9(sus4)
3
1
GMaj7
GMaj7
2
GMaj7
GMaj7

A Shade of Jade

Joe Henderson

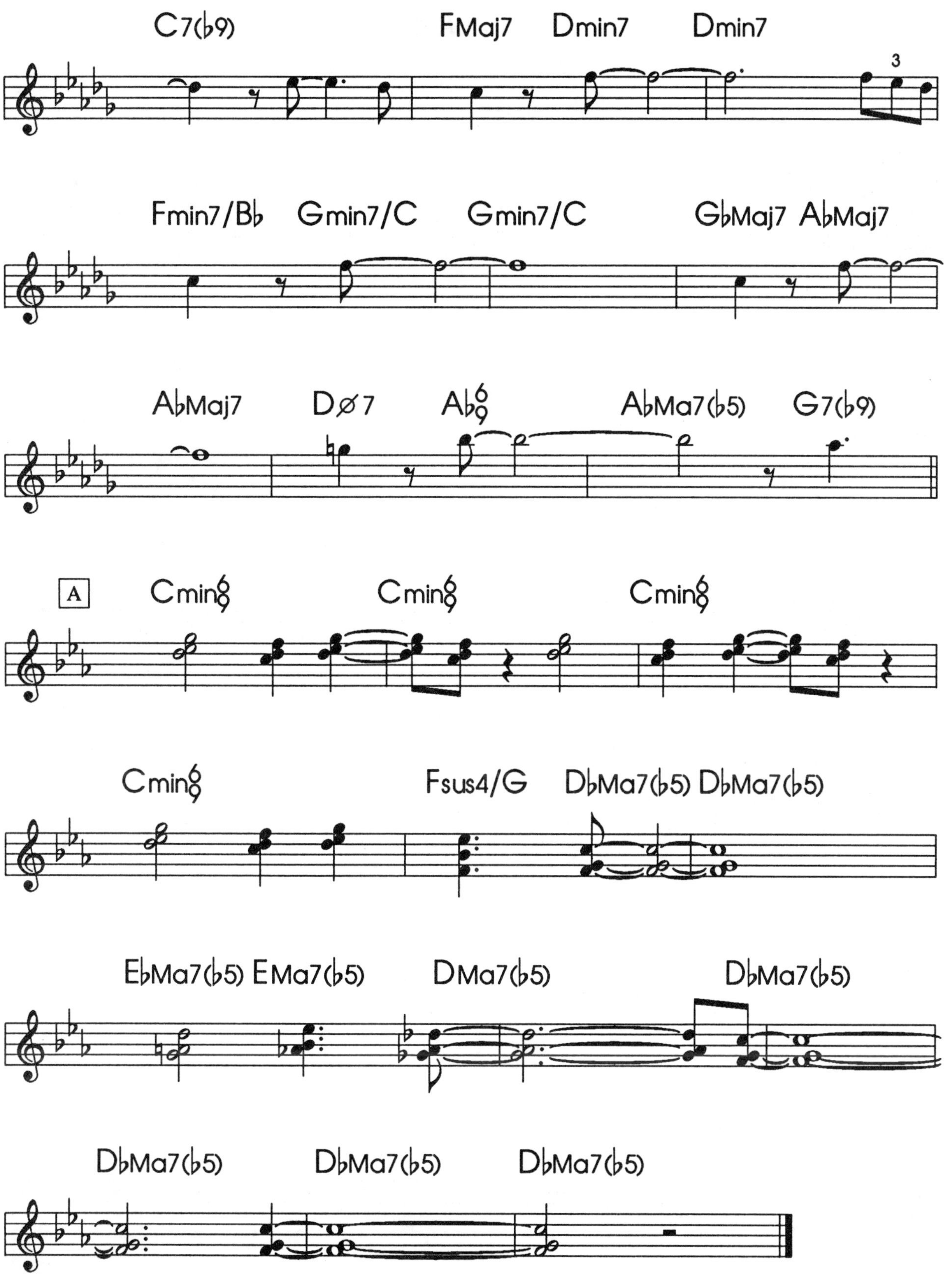
C7(♭9)
FMaj7
Dmin7
Dmin7
3
Fmin7/B♭
Gmin7/C
Gmin7/C
G♭Maj7
A♭Maj7
A♭Maj7
DØ7
A♭6/9
A♭Ma7(♭5)
G7(♭9)
A
Cmin6/9
Cmin6/9
Cmin6/9
Cmin6/9
Fsus4/G
D♭Ma7(♭5)
D♭Ma7(♭5)
E♭Ma7(♭5)
EMa7(♭5)
DMa7(♭5)
D♭Ma7(♭5)
D♭Ma7(♭5)
D♭Ma7(♭5)
D♭Ma7(♭5)

Shakey Jake

Cedar Walton

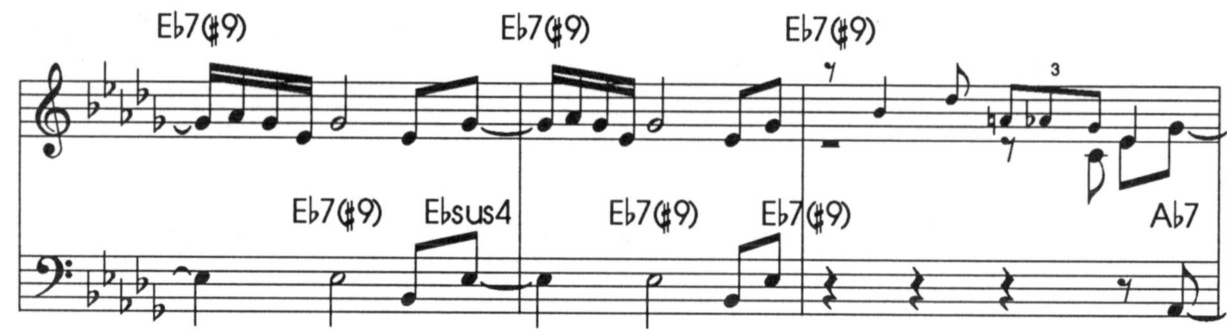

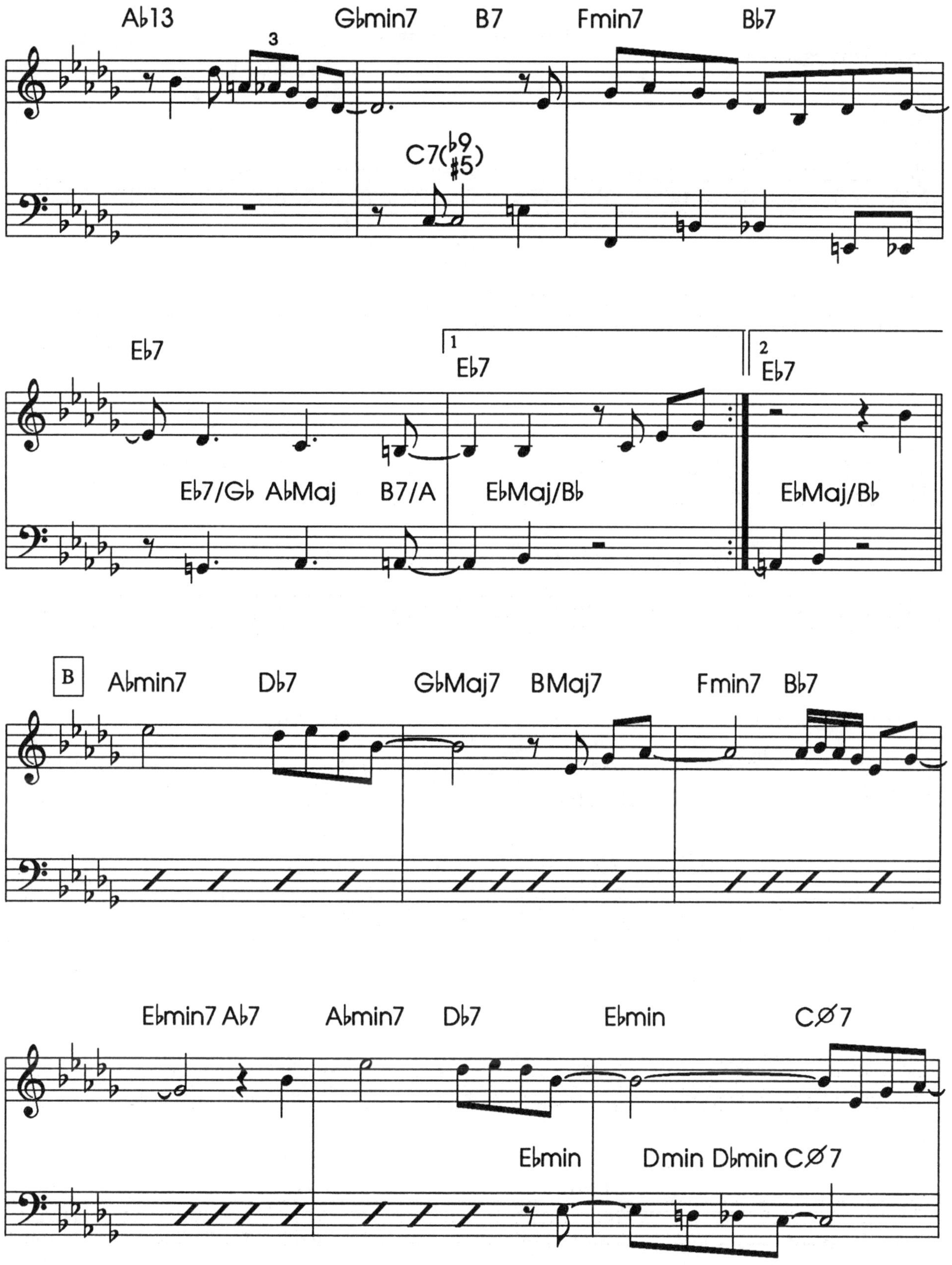

Ab13 Gbmin7 B7 Fmin7 Bb7

C7(b9 #5)

Eb7 1 Eb7 2 Eb7

Eb7/Gb AbMaj B7/A EbMaj/Bb EbMaj/Bb

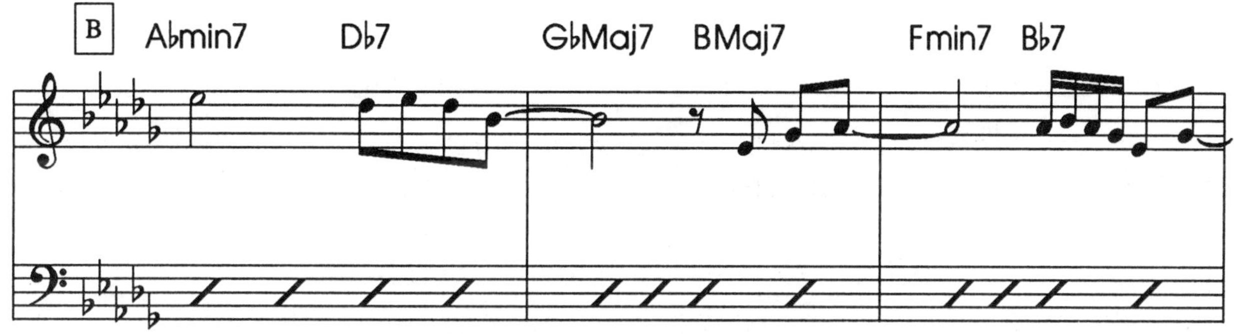

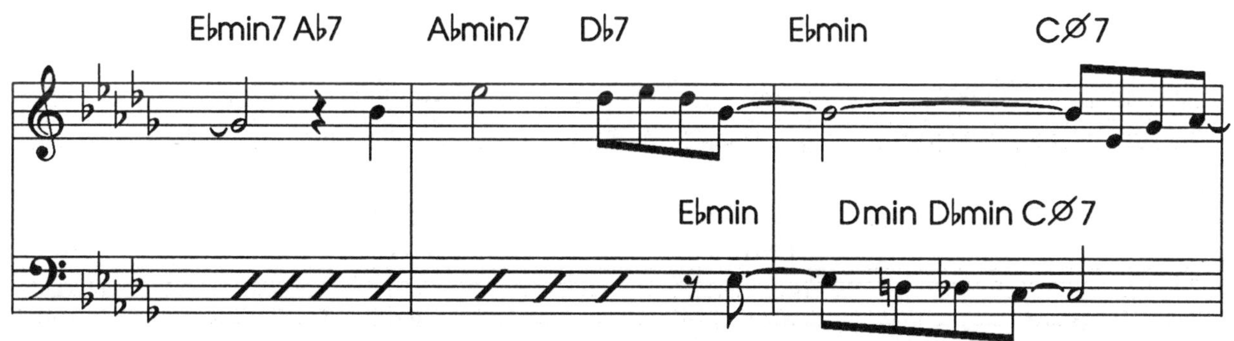

After solos, D.C. al Coda

Coda
C7(♭9 #5)
E♭7/G♭ A♭Maj B7/A
3
E♭Maj/B♭
C7(♭9 #5)
E♭7/G♭ A♭Maj B7/A
3
E♭Maj/B♭
C7(♭9 #5)
E♭7(#9)
E♭7(#9)

Snap Back Jack

Brother Jack McDuff

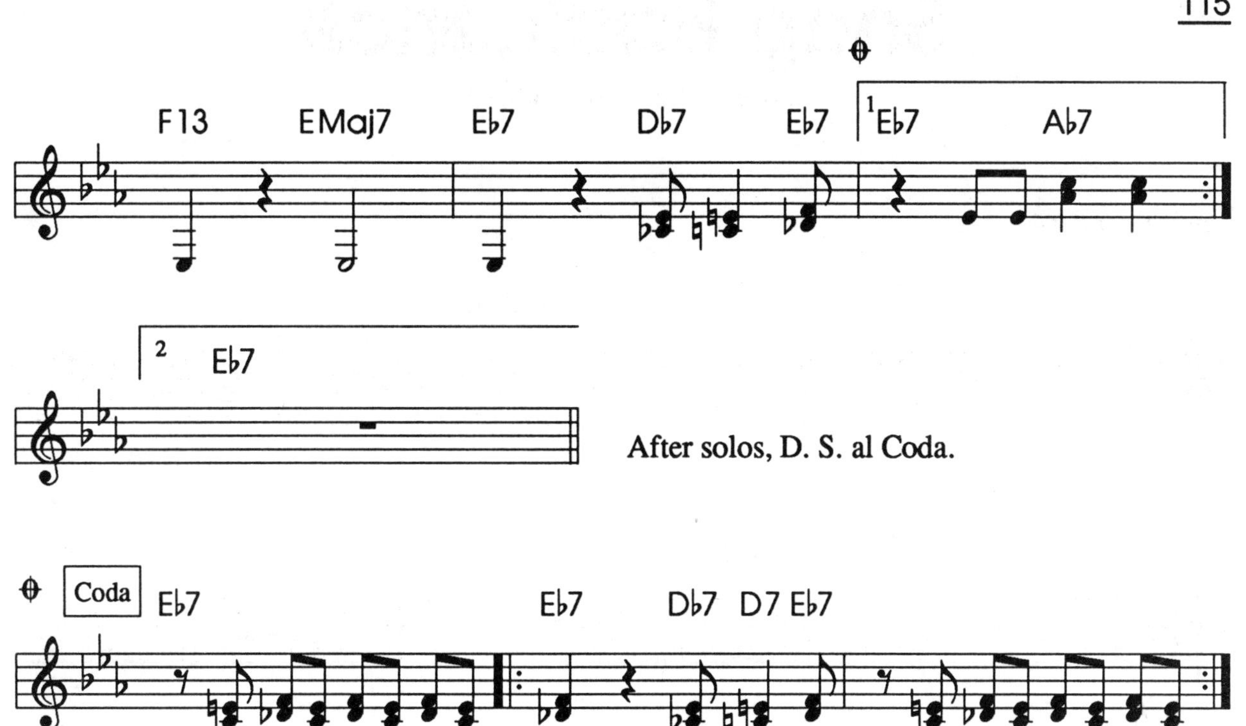

Repeat several times with keyboard solo and fade out.

Song For Darnell

Mulgrew Miller

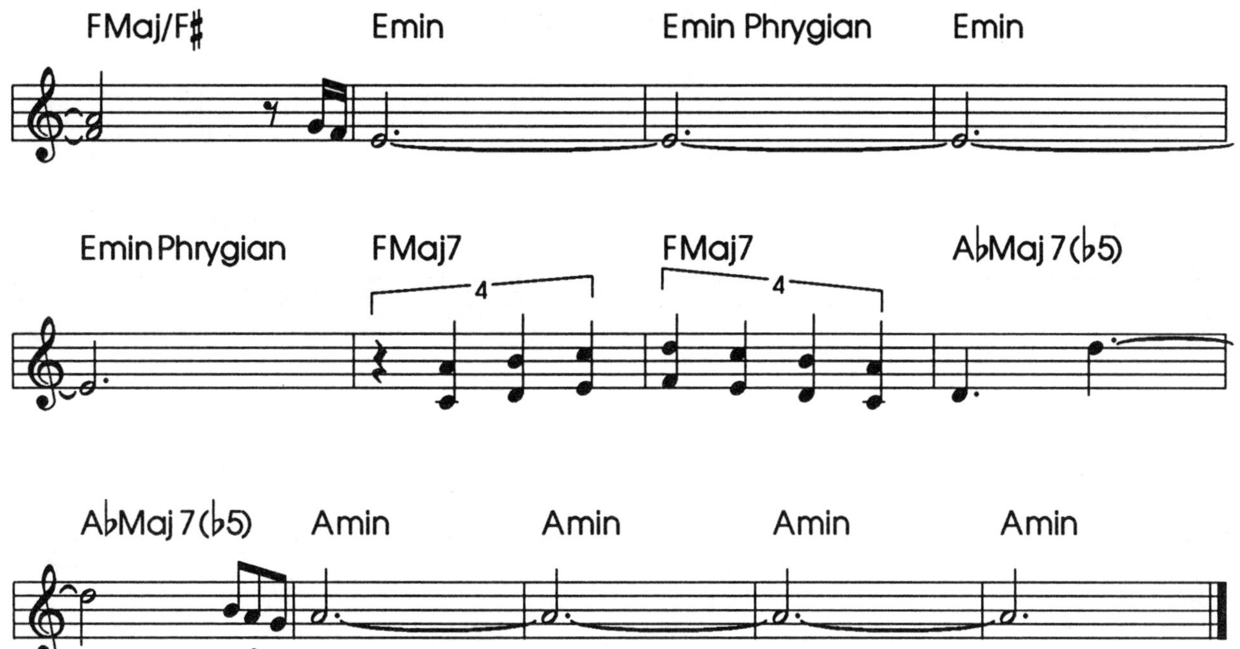
FMaj/F♯
Emin
Emin Phrygian
Emin
Emin Phrygian
FMaj7
4
FMaj7
4
A♭Maj 7(♭5)
A♭Maj 7(♭5)
3
Amin
Amin
Amin
Amin

Sortie

Curtis Fuller

(abridged version)

medium tempo

Solos on ABAC chord changes.

Spidit

Hal Galper

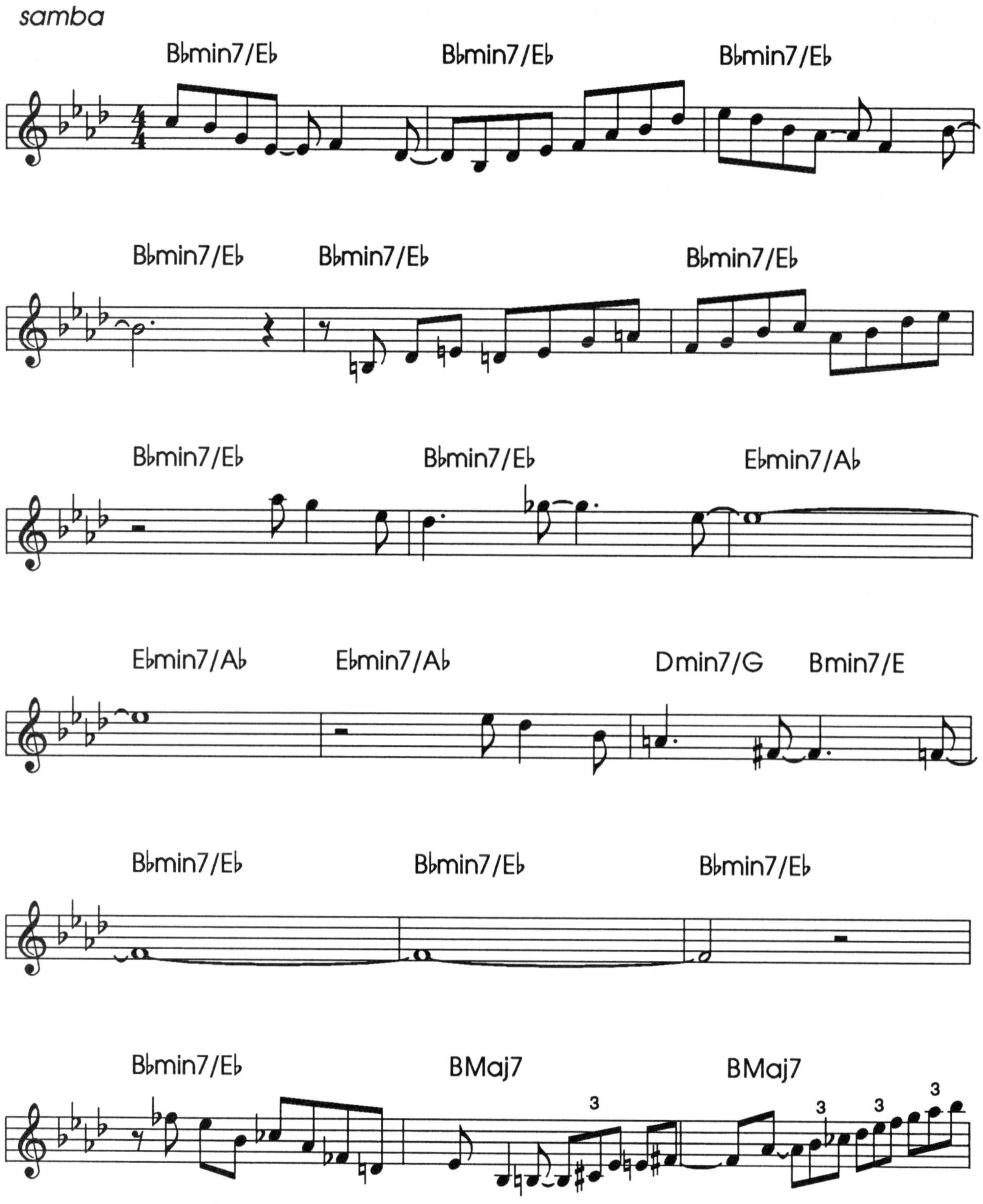

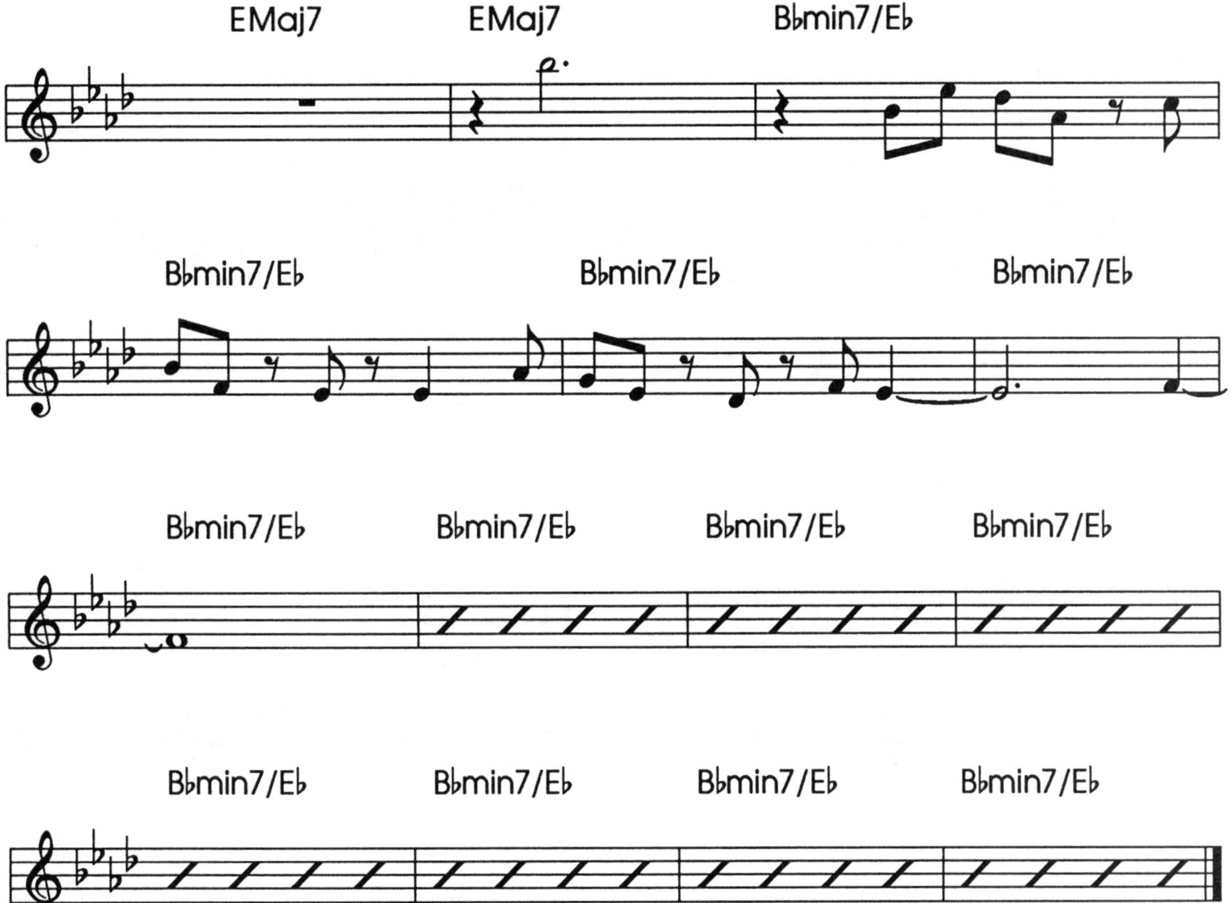
EMaj7
EMaj7
B♭min7/E♭
B♭min7/E♭
B♭min7/E♭
B♭min7/E♭
B♭min7/E♭
B♭min7/E♭
B♭min7/E♭
B♭min7/E♭
B♭min7/E♭
B♭min7/E♭
B♭min7/E♭
B♭min7/E♭

Strolling Blues

Brother Jack McDuff

medium fast blues

B♭7
Bdim7
F7
3
F7
Bdim7
B9(♭5)
B♭7
3
B♭7
Bdim7
F7
3
B♭9
Bdim7
A♭13
F7
Gmin7
C7
3
A♭13
F7
1 F7
2 F7
D13
G7(♯9)
C13
C13
After solos, D.S. al Coda.
Coda
F7(♯9)

Time's Mirror

Tom Harrell

EMaj7/B AMaj7/B EMaj7/B AMaj7/B
Ebmin7(b5) Ab7(b9 sus4) Ab7(b9) Dbmin7 Gmin7 C7(b9)
FMaj7 Dmin9 Bmin11 E7(b9) AMaj7 DMaj7 Bbmin9 Eb9
C
E7(#9 #5) E9(#5) Eb13(#9) Eb9(#5) E7(#9 #5) E9(#5) Eb13(#9) Eb9(#5)
3
CMaj7/D Bmin7/E CMaj7/D C13(#9) C7(13 9) B7(#9) B7(b9 #5)
3
Emin9(no7) G#min7 Bbmin7 Emin9(no7) Bbmin11 A9(#5)
AbMaj9 AbMaj9(#5) AMaj9 AMaj9(#5) Bmin11 Dmin11 G9

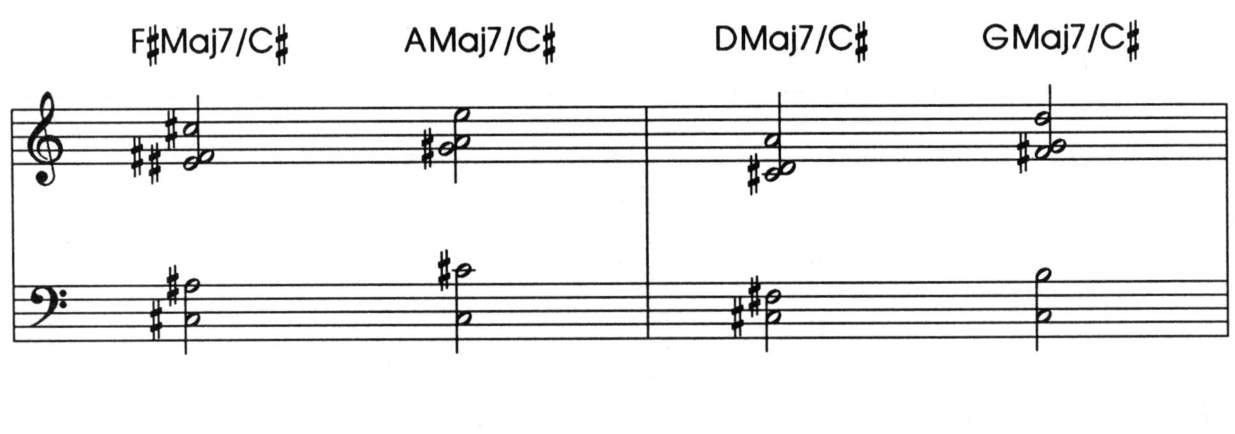

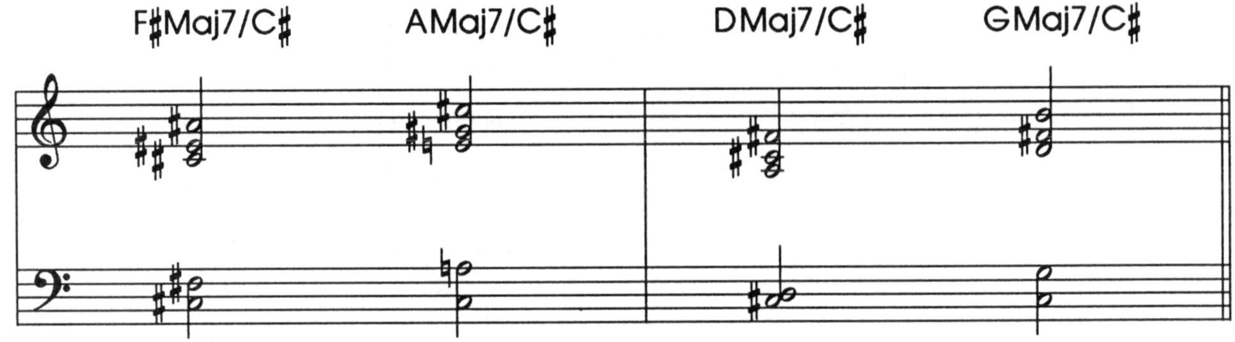

Solos on AABC chord changes. After solos, D.C. al Coda.

I'll tell you, man, I don't put nothing down. If somebody wants to play a cabbage, it's all right with me. But I'm going to stick to the wood, because those are my roots, that's the way I came up.

• Hampton Hawes

Notes and Tones by Arthur Taylor. (Perigee Books, N.Y., 1982)

Touch The Sky

Tom Harrell

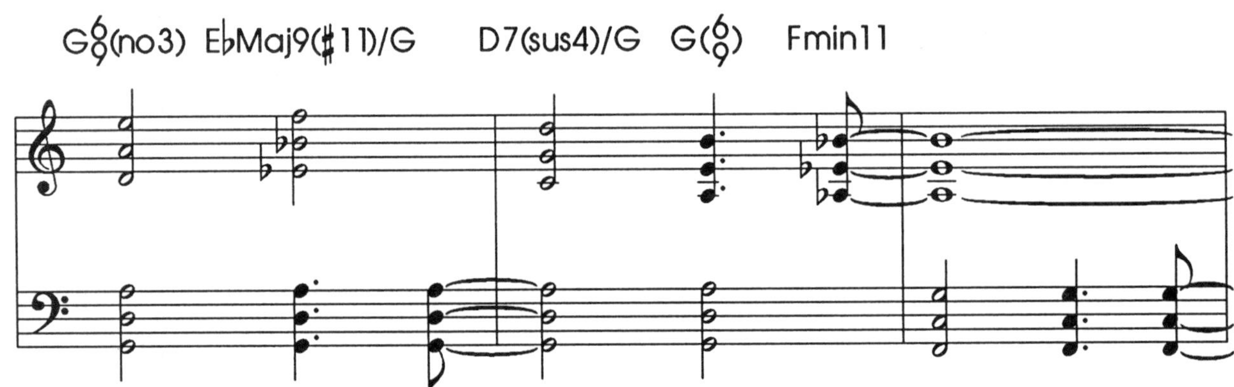

Fmin11
FMaj7(6/9)
F9(sus4)
F6/9(no3)
FMaj9(♯11)
Fmin11
Fmin11
Fmin11
FMaj7(6/9)F9(sus4)
F6/9(no3)
FMaj9(♯11)
B
E♭min11
D♭Maj7(6/9)
Cmin11
B♭min11
Gmin11
Gmin11
Fmin11
E♭Maj7(6/9)
Dmin11
Cmin11

Amin11 Bmin11
D7(♭13 ♯9 ♭9)
B♭13(sus4)
B♭13(sus4)
E7(♭13 ♯9) B7(♭13 ♯9)
Amin7(♯5) Gmin7(♯5)
B♭13(sus4)
B♭13(sus4)
E7(♭13 ♯9) B7(♭13 ♯9)
Amin7(♯5) Gmin7(♯5)
A♭13(sus4) B13(sus4)
B13(sus4)
DMaj7(♯5) AMaj7(♯5)
1
GMaj7(♯5) Fmin7(♯5)
2
GMaj7(♯5) Fmin7(♯5) G♭Maj7(add6)
C
Swing
Gmin7(♯5)

Gmin7(♯5)
D♭Maj7/A♭
D7(♯9)/A
E♭Maj7/B♭
G7(♯5 ♭5)
G7(♭13 ♯9)
C9(sus4)
C13
C9
Cmin7
FMaj6
F9
FMaj6
F9
AMaj7(♯11 9 6)
AMaj7(♯11 9 6)
AMaj7(♯11 9 6)
D
Gmin11
(8)
Fmin11
(8)
Horn Solos first time, Piano solo second time
E♭min11
Cmin11
Gmin11
Gmin11

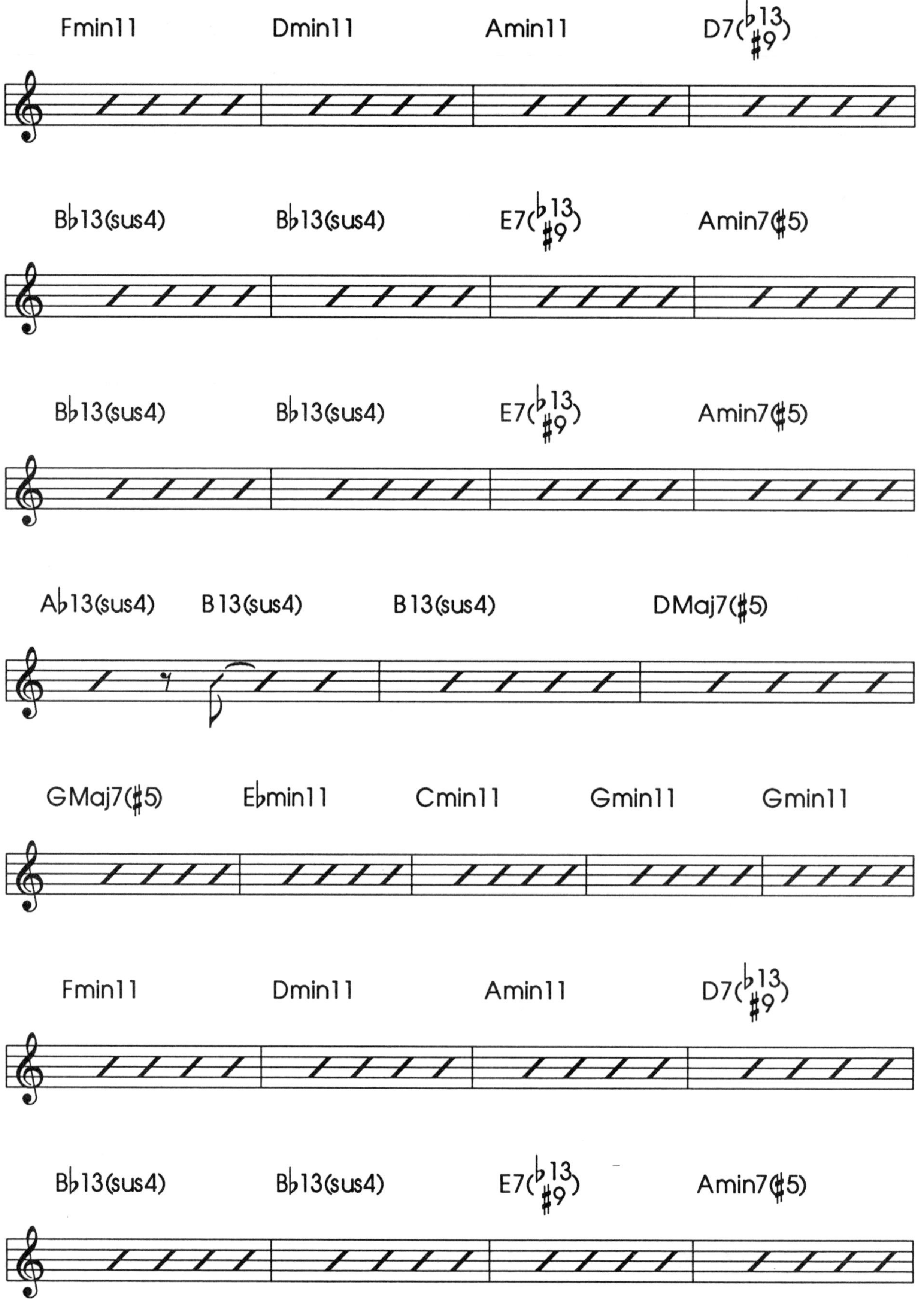
Fmin11
Dmin11
Amin11
D7(♭13 ♯9)
B♭13(sus4)
B♭13(sus4)
E7(♭13 ♯9)
Amin7(♯5)
B♭13(sus4)
B♭13(sus4)
E7(♭13 ♯9)
Amin7(♯5)
A♭13(sus4)
B13(sus4)
B13(sus4)
DMaj7(♯5)
GMaj7(♯5)
E♭min11
Cmin11
Gmin11
Gmin11
Fmin11
Dmin11
Amin11
D7(♭13 ♯9)
B♭13(sus4)
B♭13(sus4)
E7(♭13 ♯9)
Amin7(♯5)

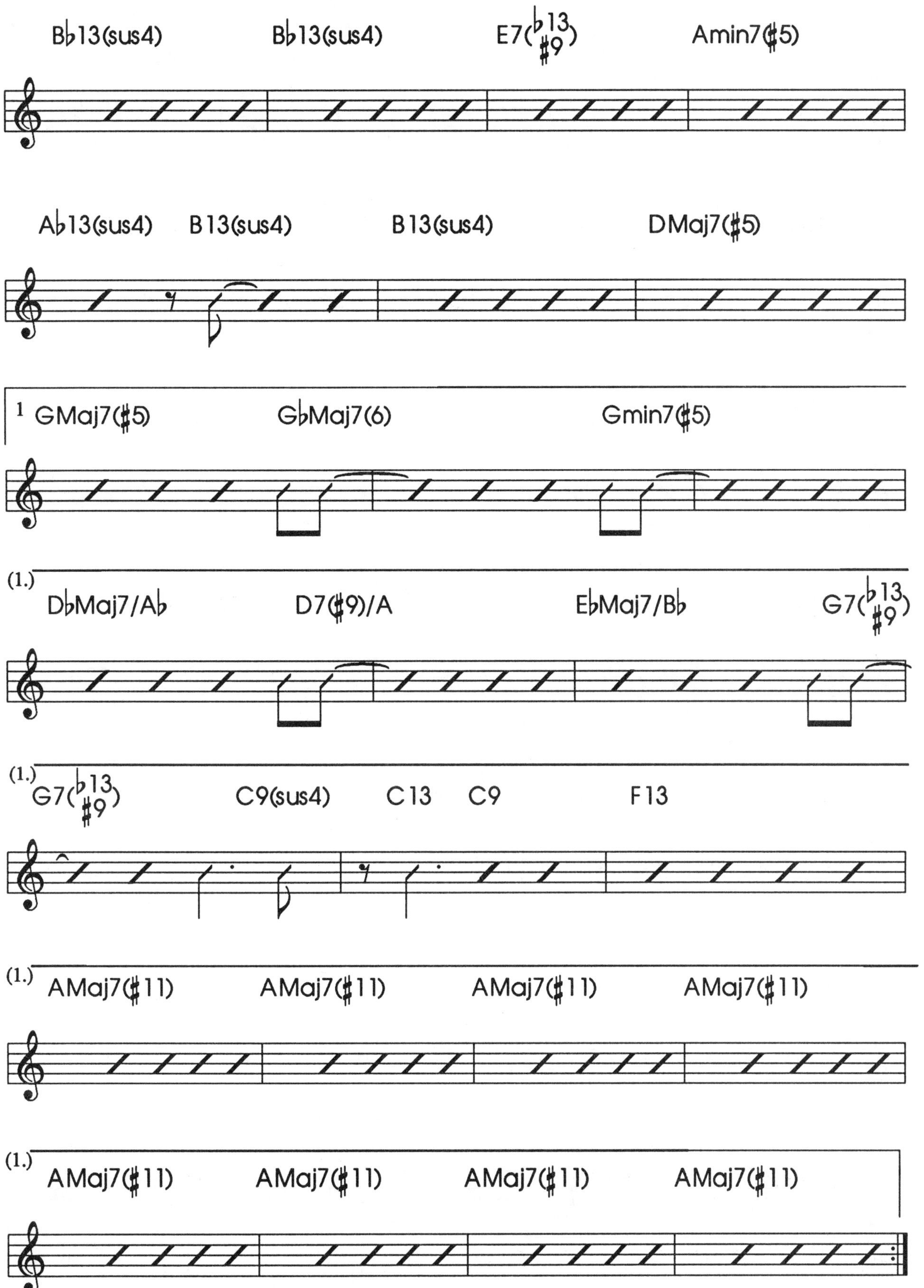
B♭13(sus4)
B♭13(sus4)
E7(♭13 ♯9)
Amin7(♯5)
A♭13(sus4)
B13(sus4)
B13(sus4)
DMaj7(♯5)
1
GMaj7(♯5)
G♭Maj7(6)
Gmin7(♯5)
(1.)
D♭Maj7/A♭
D7(♯9)/A
E♭Maj7/B♭
G7(♭13 ♯9)
(1.)
G7(♭13 ♯9)
C9(sus4)
C13
C9
F13
(1.)
AMaj7(♯11)
AMaj7(♯11)
AMaj7(♯11)
AMaj7(♯11)
(1.)
AMaj7(♯11)
AMaj7(♯11)
AMaj7(♯11)
AMaj7(♯11)

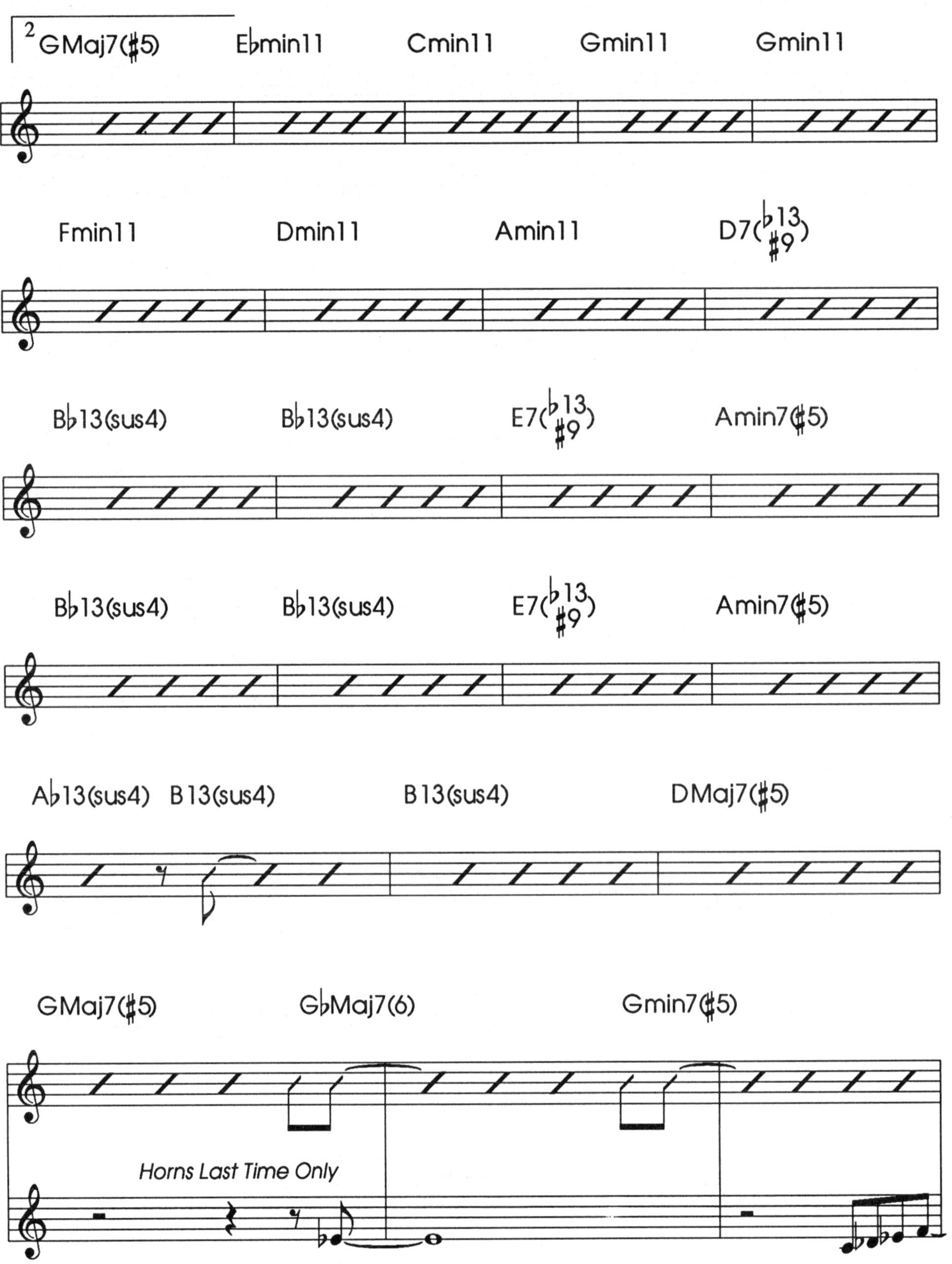
2
GMaj7(♯5)
E♭min11
Cmin11
Gmin11
Gmin11
Fmin11
Dmin11
Amin11
D7(♭13 ♯9)
B♭13(sus4)
B♭13(sus4)
E7(♭13 ♯9)
Amin7(♯5)
B♭13(sus4)
B♭13(sus4)
E7(♭13 ♯9)
Amin7(♯5)
A♭13(sus4)
B13(sus4)
B13(sus4)
DMaj7(♯5)
GMaj7(♯5)
G♭Maj7(6)
Gmin7(♯5)
Horns Last Time Only

DbMaj7/Ab
D7(#9)/A
EbMaj7/Bb
G7(#5 b5)
G7(#5 b5)
G7(b13 #9)
C9(sus4)
C13
C9
Cmin7
FMaj6
F9
FMaj6
F9
AMaj7(#11 9 6)
Break
After piano solo, D.C. al Coda
Coda
EbMaj7/Bb
G7(#5 b5)
G7(b13 #9)
C9(sus4)
C13
C9
Cmin7
FMaj6
F9
FMaj6
F9
AMaj7(#11 9 6)

Triple Play

Hal Galper

Intro and Interlude (Piano fill)
Open Until Cue

EMaj7
EMaj7
CMaj7
CMaj7
A♭Maj7
A♭Maj7
CMaj7
CMaj7
A♭Maj7
F♯Maj7
EMaj7
E♭Maj
D♭7
Cmin7
F7
Fmin7
B♭7(♭9 sus4)
D♭Maj/E♭
BMaj/E♭
AMaj/E♭
BMaj/E♭
D♭Maj/E♭
BMaj/E♭
AMaj/E♭
BMaj/E♭
Interlude: Vamp Until Cue
4
BMaj/E♭
D♭Maj/E♭

Tune of the Unknown Samba

Hal Galper

G7 CMaj7 FMaj7 F♯ø7

B7(♭9) EMaj7 FMaj7 EMaj7

E♭7(♯5) A♭Maj7 A♭Maj7(♯5) D♭Maj7

D♭Maj7(♯5) G♭Maj7 B♭7(♭9) E♭min7

D♭min7 Cø7 Cø7 F7(♭9)

F7(♭9) B♭min7 E7(♯11) B♭min7/E♭ E♭7(♯5)

After solos, D.S. al Coda.

Coda

Repeat 4 times.
Ritard last time.

F7(♭9) F7(♭9) B♭min7

E♭7 E♭min7/A♭

Upswing

Tom Harrell

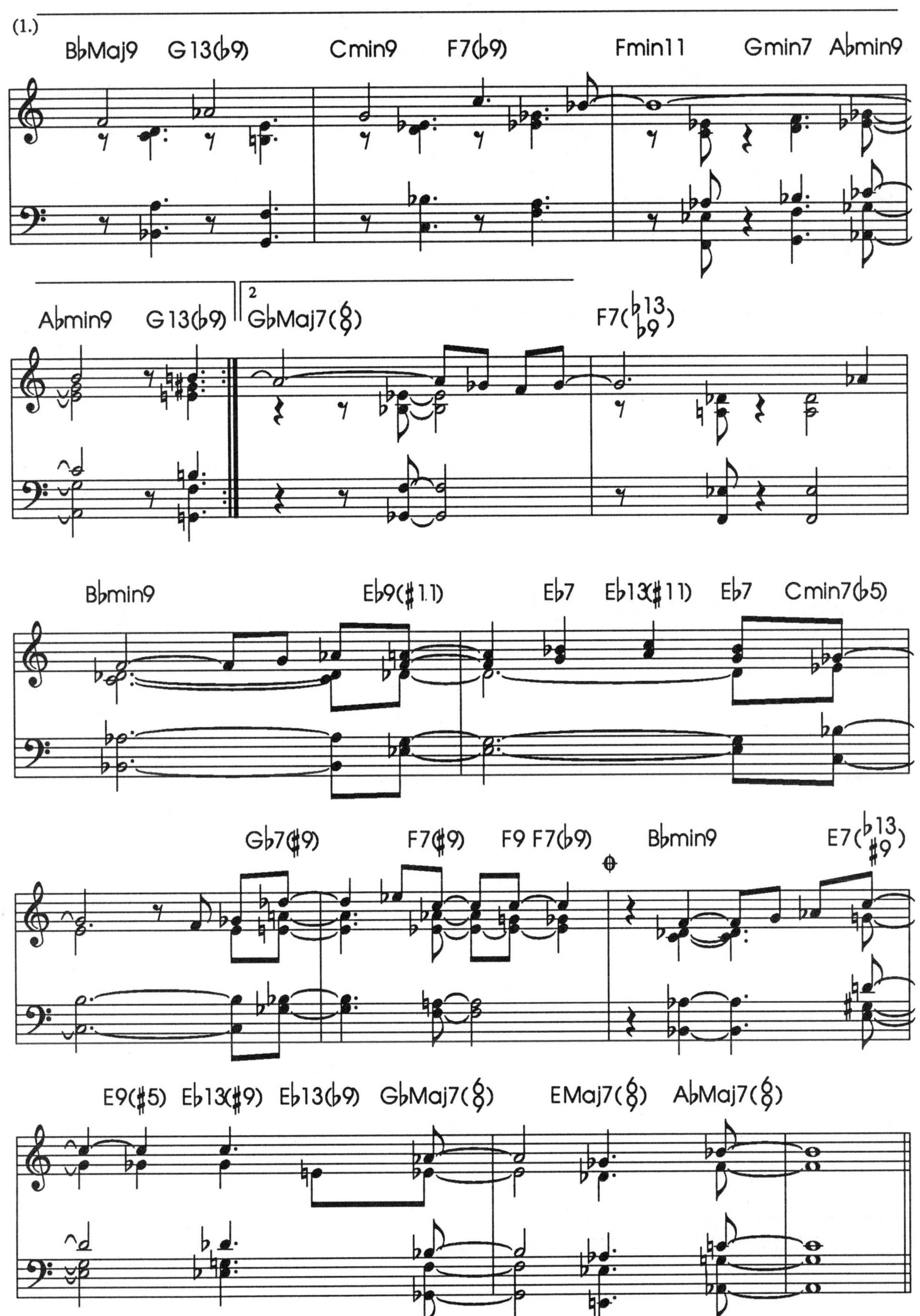
(1.)
B♭Maj9 G13(♭9) Cmin9 F7(♭9) Fmin11 Gmin7 A♭min9
A♭min9 G13(♭9)
2
G♭Maj7(6/9) F7(♭13/♭9)
B♭min9 E♭9(♯11) E♭7 E♭13(♯11) E♭7 Cmin7(♭5)
G♭7(♯9) F7(♯9) F9 F7(♭9) B♭min9 E7(♭13/♯9)
E9(♯5) E♭13(♯9) E♭13(♭9) G♭Maj7(6/9) EMaj7(6/9) A♭Maj7(6/9)

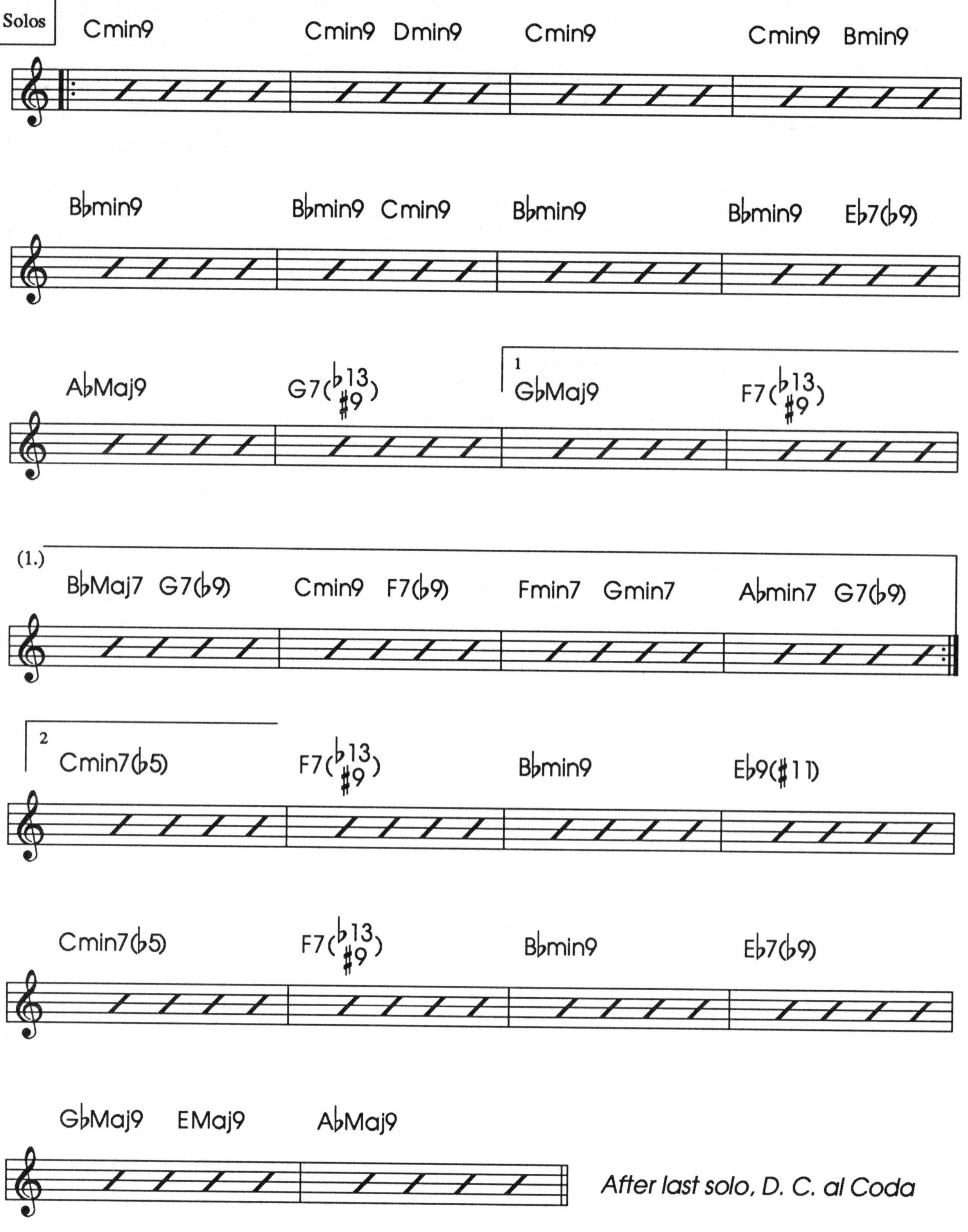
Solos
Cmin9
Cmin9 Dmin9
Cmin9
Cmin9 Bmin9
B♭min9
B♭min9 Cmin9
B♭min9
B♭min9 E♭7(♭9)
A♭Maj9
G7(♭13 ♯9)
1
G♭Maj9
F7(♭13 ♯9)
(1.)
B♭Maj7 G7(♭9)
Cmin9 F7(♭9)
Fmin7 Gmin7
A♭min7 G7(♭9)
2
Cmin7(♭5)
F7(♭13 ♯9)
B♭min9
E♭9(♯11)
Cmin7(♭5)
F7(♭13 ♯9)
B♭min9
E♭7(♭9)
G♭Maj9 EMaj9
A♭Maj9
After last solo, D. C. al Coda

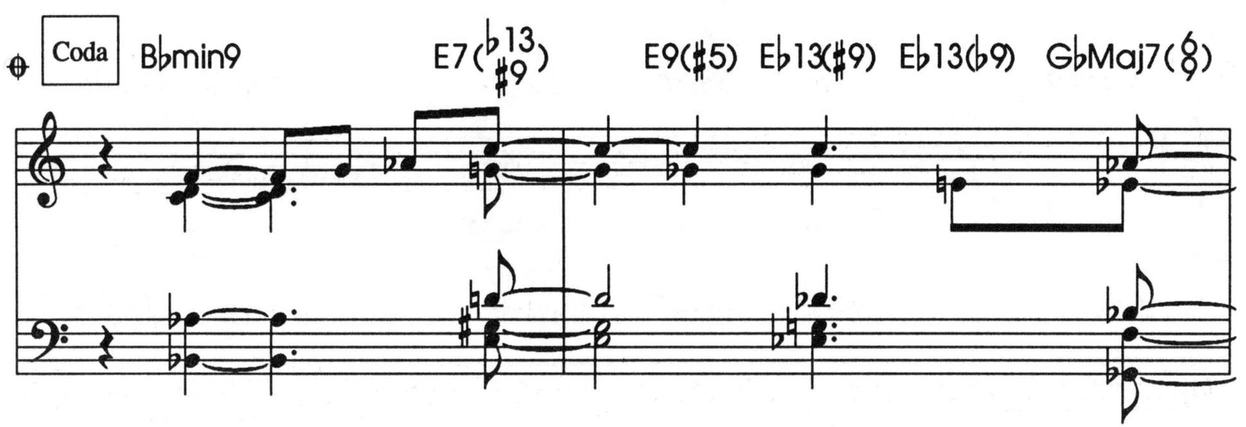
Coda
B♭min9
E7(♭13 ♯9)
E9(♯5)
E♭13(♯9)
E♭13(♭9)
G♭Maj7(6 9)

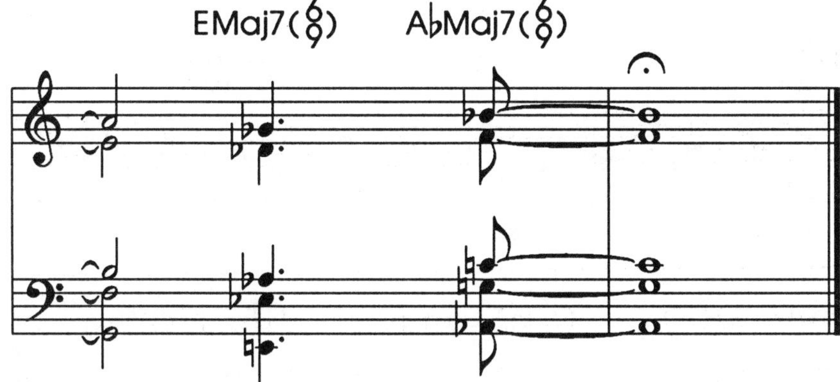
EMaj7(6 9)
A♭Maj7(6 9)

Viable Blues

Tom Harrell

G7(sus4)
C7(sus4)
C7
3
Bb9(sus4)
A9(sus4)
A2
Eb7(sus4)
Ab9(sus4)
DMaj7(6)
AbMaj7(#11)
GMaj7(#11)
Eb7(sus4)
Bbmin7(#5)
A13
3
Ab9(sus4)

After last solo, D.S. al Coda

Waiting for Chet

Hal Galper

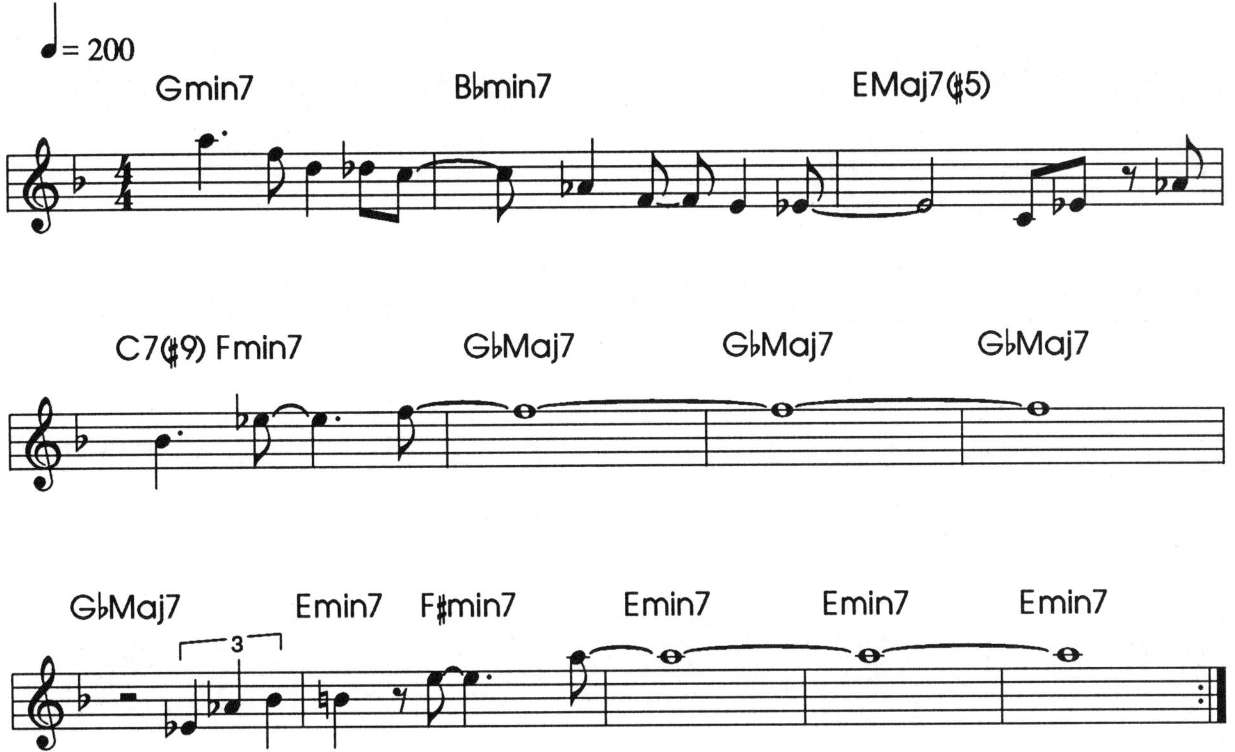

Visions of Gaudi

Tom Harrell

Dmin9(no7)
C♯min9(no7)
A2
Dmin9(no7)
A/C♯
Cmin7
Bmin7
E7(♭9)
AMaj7
F♯min7
E♭min7
A♭min7(♯5)
A♭7
D♭Maj(6/9)
E♭7(♯9/♯5)
B
E♭min7
Bmin7
Emin7
Amin7
D9
D♭Maj(6/9)
Dmin7
G13
CMaj7
G♭7(♯11)
Fmin7
B♭13
Dmin9(no7)
C♯min9(no7)
2
2

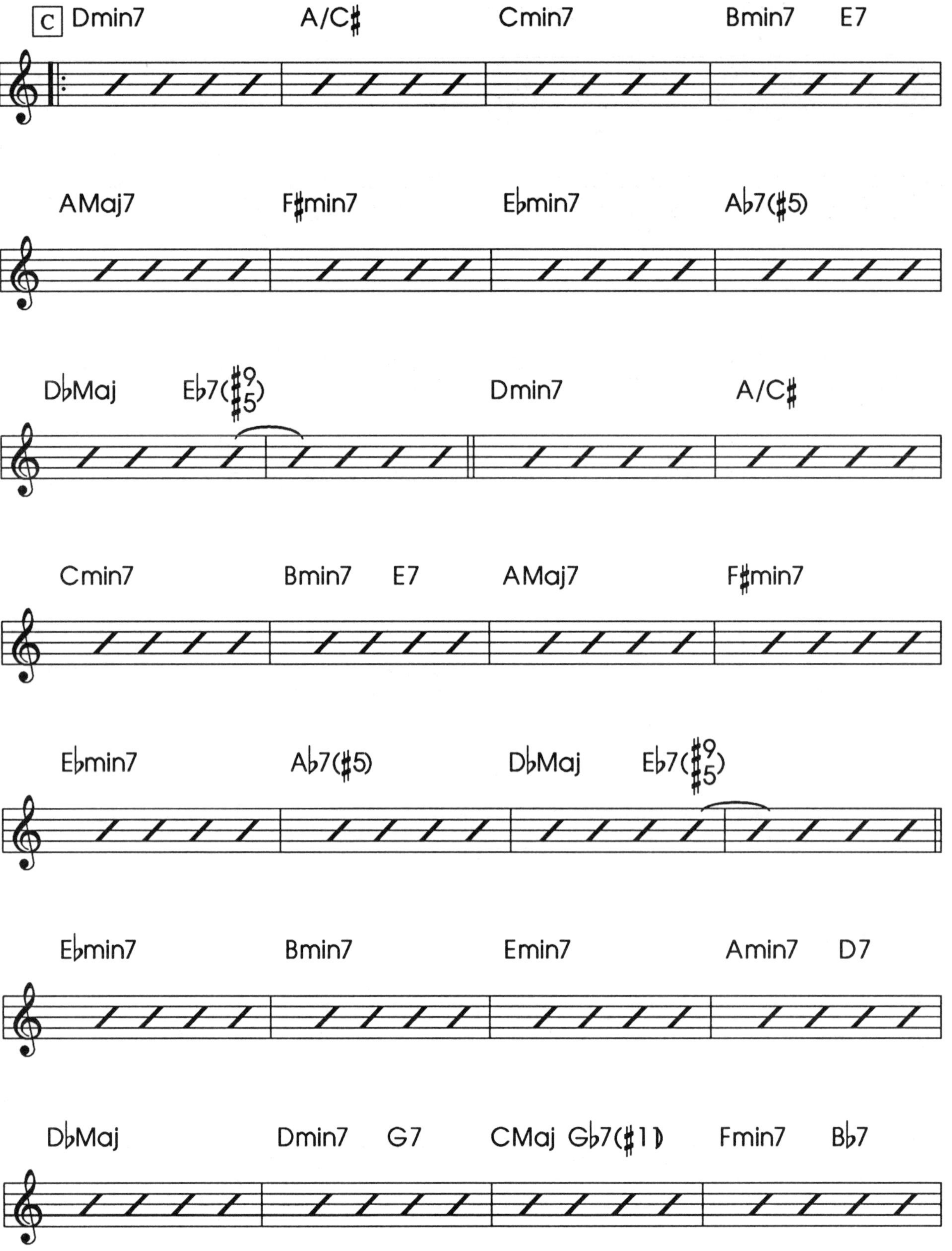
C
Dmin7
A/C♯
Cmin7
Bmin7
E7
AMaj7
F♯min7
E♭min7
A♭7(♯5)
D♭Maj
E♭7(♯9 ♯5)
Dmin7
A/C♯
Cmin7
Bmin7
E7
AMaj7
F♯min7
E♭min7
A♭7(♯5)
D♭Maj
E♭7(♯9 ♯5)
E♭min7
Bmin7
Emin7
Amin7
D7
D♭Maj
Dmin7
G7
CMaj
G♭7(♯11)
Fmin7
B♭7

Dmin9(no7)
C♯min9(no7)
2
2
2
2
2
2
D.S. al Coda

Coda
Dmin9(no7)
C♯min9(no7)
FMaj EMaj D♭Maj CMaj AMaj A♭Maj FMaj
EMaj
C♯min13

Weaver

Tom Harrell

medium swing

B
B♭/C
Bmin7(♯5)
B♭9(sus4)
A7(♯5)
A♭13(♯11)
A♭13(♯11)
C9(sus4)
F7(sus4)
F7(sus4)
C
A♭Maj7(6/9)
G♭Maj7(6/9)
3
A♭Maj7(6/9)
G♭Maj7(6/9)

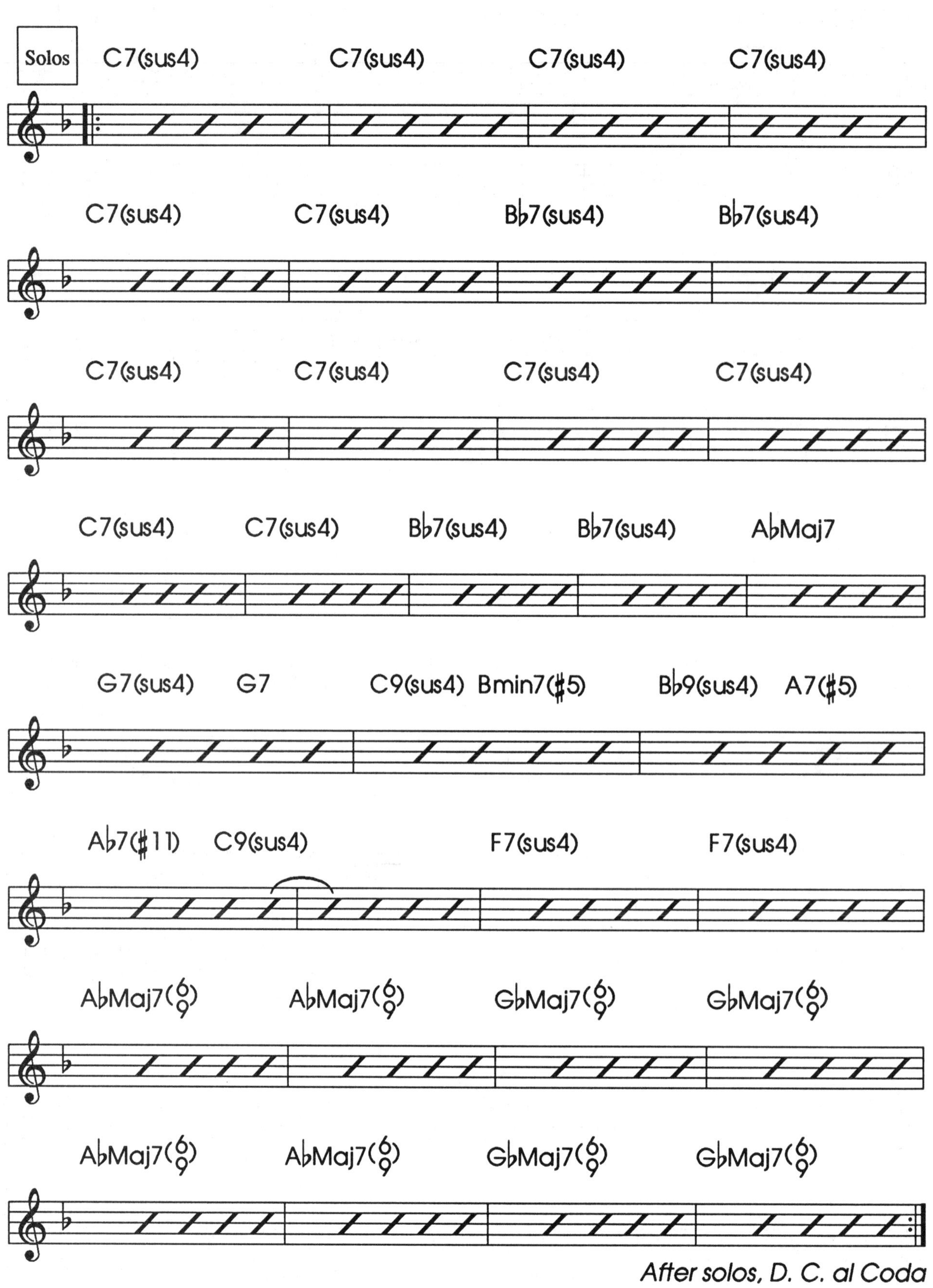

After solos, D. C. al Coda

(No Repeat on D.C.)

Coda
C7(sus4)/F
C7(sus4)/F
C7(sus4)/F
C7(sus4)/F
C7(sus4)/F
C7(sus4)/F
B♭7(sus4)
B♭7(sus4)
C7(sus4)/F
C7(sus4)/F
C7(sus4)/F
C7(sus4)/F
C7(sus4)/F
C7(sus4)/F
B♭7(sus4)
B♭7(sus4)
A♭Maj6
G7
G♭Maj7

When Love Is New

Cedar Walton

Solos on A only. After solos, skip to B. The piece ends with a restatement of the Intro, with the pickup to A omitted.

Zoltan

Woody Shaw

CMaj7(♭5)
CMaj7(♭5)
B♭Maj7(♭5)
B♭Maj7(♭5)
Doubletime swing
B
A♭13
A♭13
G13
F13
F13
Doubletime mambo
A
CMaj7(♭5)
CMaj7(♭5)
B♭Maj7(♭5)
B♭Maj7(♭5)
Solo on ABA chord changes then go on to C.
C
march
Organ:
D.S. al Coda
Coda
Drum Solo
4
Fade out

Index